2016 CLEVELAND IS
KING!

BRENDAN BOWERS   **FOREWORD BY MARK PRICE**

This book is book is available in quantity at special discounts for your group or organization.
For further information, contact:

Triumph Books LLC
814 North Franklin Street
Chicago, Illinois 60610
Phone: (312) 337-0747
www.triumphbooks.com

Printed in U.S.A.
ISBN: 978-1-62937-218-1

Content packaged by Mojo Media, Inc.
Joe Funk: Editor
Jason Hinman: Creative Director

All interior photos by AP Images

Front cover photo by USA TODAY Sports. Back cover photo by AP Images.

CONTENTS

Foreword *by Mark Price* 4

NBA Finals vs. Golden State 8

Ending the Championship Drought 34

Regular Season 40

LeBron James 50

Kyrie Irving 58

Kevin Love 66

J.R. Smith 72

Tristan Thompson 76

Richard Jefferson 80

Tyronn Lue 84

Eastern Conference Quarterfinals vs. Detroit 88

Eastern Conference Semifinals vs. Atlanta 96

Eastern Conference Finals vs. Toronto 104

FOREWORD

By Mark Price

The fans of the Cleveland Cavaliers have always been all in. When I first joined the Cavs in 1986, the togetherness of the Northeast Ohio community stood out immediately. The love and support Cleveland fans have for their team is both genuine and real—and it still is to this day. I was blessed to feel that love firsthand as a player, and it fueled everything my teammates and I accomplished out on the floor. Thirty years later, I'm still blessed to be part of the Cleveland Cavaliers community. Only this time—in support of this year's team—I was all in myself, rooting right alongside the great fans of Northeast Ohio during this magical run.

Being a Cleveland Cavalier was an awesome experience. The fans used to rock the Richfield Coliseum so loudly that we never thought we'd ever lose a home game. In the playoffs, that excitement from inside the arena could be felt all over the city. It was a special time, and a special place, in a special community. It brought back great memories for me to see that same electric spirit come alive in Cleveland all over again this season—especially now that I'm coaching the Charlotte 49ers and no longer forced to face the Cavs as an opposing NBA coach.

The big man duo of Kevin Love and Tristan Thompson, meanwhile, were instrumental in carrying the Cavs' frontcourt throughout the playoffs and the Finals. Love piled up double-doubles early in the playoffs and showed off his ever-evolving and impressively versatile offensive game. Thompson made his presence known most notably in the Finals, playing big minutes, dominating the glass, and protecting the rim with ferocity. He's a guy who never gets the credit he deserves. He does the dirty work that championships require every night.

Beyond the statistical accomplishments, LeBron's greatest achievement this season—in my opinion, at least—was the way that he led his teammates. He challenged them when they needed to be challenged early on in the season, but he also supported them all the way. By the time the playoffs began, it was evident how close this team had truly become. They shared the ball brilliantly. They defended as a unit. Everyone knew their role and everyone executed. That camaraderie and togetherness was instilled and fostered by LeBron, and it elevated the performance of their team at just the right moment.

As a point guard, I was also proud of the way that Kyrie Irving played throughout the postseason. He managed his role as a floor general and potent scorer perfectly, and played with great balance. I've always thought he was underrated as far as being compared

LeBron James and his teammates not only made Cavs history with their championship but delivered the first title to Cleveland in 52 years.

to the top point guards in the league, and I think he proved that throughout this run. He found his niche with his teammates, played with a lot of confidence, and was truly terrific on nightly basis.

Kevin Love, meanwhile, really showed how far the Cavaliers might have gone last season if he hadn't been injured. He was a double-double machine who is uniquely able to spread the floor effectively with his outside shot. I've also always been impressed with Kevin's versatility as a big man. He excelled on the interior early on in his career in Minnesota, and then excelled again as more of a stretch-four in Cleveland. The Cavaliers really relied on not only his points and rebounds, but also the driving lanes he creates with his shot. Throughout this run, he delivered in all areas at an All-Star caliber level.

In addition to the Big Three—along with an excellent job of game-planning, strategy and coaching by Tyronn Lue and his staff—this Cavaliers team was able excel on the game's biggest stage because their role players showed up in a major way. Tristan Thompson is a guy who never gets the credit he deserves. He does the dirty work that championships require every night, and remained a constant threat on the offensive glass throughout. J.R. Smith hit big shots. Matthew Dellavedova provided a spark on both ends of the floor. Richard Jefferson, Channing Frye, all the guys, they played with the team-first attitude and winning spirit of true professionals.

It was beautiful to watch all of the pieces and players come together for a team who worked so hard to make that a reality this season. They are a team this city deserves and I'll never forget the memories they provided. As a former player, I was proud to watch this

group represent not only the city, but also Austin Carr, Brad Daugherty, Larry Nance, Zydrunas Ilgauskas and all the great Cavaliers who came before them in the way that they did. But if I'm most excited about any one thing, it's that Cleveland has finally become what I've always known it to be—the home of champions.

Mark Price
June, 2016

Mark Price spent nine seasons with the Cavaliers, where he was a four-time All-Star, one-time All-NBA First Team, and had his number 25 retired. He is currently the head coach of the University of North Carolina at Charlotte 49ers men's basketball team.

Tyronn Lue was overcome with emotion after the Cavs clinched the title, culminating an amazing journey for the rookie head coach and former journeyman backup point guard.

NBA FINALS

GAME 1: WARRIORS 104, CAVALIERS 89
June 2, 2016 · Oakland, California

DAZED AND CONFUSED

The Cavs Contain Curry and Thompson But Still Lose by 15

The Cleveland Cavaliers arrived on the NBA Finals stage determined to not let the All-Star backcourt of Stephen Curry and Klay Thompson beat them. During Game 1 against the Golden State Warriors, Cleveland accomplished that goal.

The Splash Brothers combined to score a season-low 20 points, finishing 8 of 27 from the floor. Unfortunately for the Cavs, however, they were simply destroyed by every other professional baller in the Bay who entered the game. The Warriors' bench outscored the Cavaliers' reserves 45-10, while starters Harrison Barnes (13 points) and Andrew Bogut (10 points) also eclipsed their season scoring averages. This effort defensively, coupled with Cleveland missing 28 shots in the paint and appearing thoroughly confused on offense, helped the Warriors cruise to a 1-0 series advantage with the 104-89 win in Oakland.

On a night where Cleveland's Big 3 of LeBron James (23 points), Kyrie Irving (26 points) and Kevin Love (17 points) combined to outscore Curry, Thompson and Draymond Green 66-36, Golden State's supporting cast proved its championship mettle.

Longtime veterans Shaun Livingston and Leandro Barbosa exploded off the bench to stun the Cavaliers with 31 points on a nearly perfect 13-of-15 shooting performance. Livingston, specifically—one of seven Warriors in double figures for the game—used his 6-7 height advantage at the point guard position to elevate over his smaller defenders while feasting on mid-range jumpers to total a game-high 20 points.

Despite a third quarter rally, the Cavaliers trailed by nine points at halftime before losing by 15 in a game that they trailed by as many as 20.

"Well, I mean, we went up three, and I thought we did a great job of fighting our way back and staying the course," Tyronn Lue said postgame of the 15-0 run the Cavaliers used to first take a 68-67 lead in a back-and-forth third quarter. "You know, in the first half we struggled a little bit offensively. I just thought in the second half we came back in that third quarter, really got physical, really got aggressive, and we were able to take a three-point lead."

The glimmer of hope that third quarter lead provided was quickly extinguished by a 14-0 Warriors run to help seal the victory. Lue's high-octane offense that roared through the Eastern Conference was thrown off the rails by defending champion coach Steve Kerr for far too much of the night. The Warriors switched all screens defensively, forcing the Cavs into isolation basketball and they willingly took the bait.

Cleveland and its coaching staff also failed to recognize where double-teams were being sent in the half-court, resulting in a disjointed attack that led to shot after shot over multiple defenders. Starting guard J.R. Smith only attempted three field goals for the game, and Channing Frye was questionably glued to a Cleveland bench that was totally dominated despite his production throughout the playoffs.

"We're not a team that loses our composure over anything," James said following the Game 1 loss. "We played well in the third quarter to get ourselves back into the game, even taking the lead a couple times. It

Kevin Love, center, reaches for the ball between Warriors center Andrew Bogut, left, and forward Draymond Green during the first half of Game 1 of the NBA Finals. Love had an effective game in a losing effort, with 17 points and 13 rebounds.

was a six-point game to start the fourth, and we just didn't start the quarter like we should have, and they did a great job of pushing the lead up to double digits really fast."

The silver lining for Cleveland heading into Game 2 was that it appeared most of the mistakes they made were correctable. They finished with only 17 assists as a team—compared to 29 by Golden State—and uncharacteristically turned it over 15 times leading to easy baskets at the other end.

With two days in between games, the Cavaliers would have an opportunity to watch film and make the necessary adjustments. They were certainly capable of

moving the basketball more effectively, converting the dozens of missed shots from point-blank range, and holding the likes of Livingston and company in check. If they could accomplish all of this, while not allowing Curry and Thompson to catch fire, the Cavs could still steal home court and send the series back to Cleveland at 1-1 even after the disappointing loss.

"Those two guys are great players so we know that they will come out with an even more aggressive mindset," Irving said of Thompson and Curry heading into Game 2. "Their bench did an incredible job coming in. We just have to limit those guys and have an aggressive mindset with our second unit as well." ■

NBA FINALS

GAME 2: WARRIORS 110, CAVALIERS 77
June 5, 2016 · Oakland, California

REELING

Cavs Fall Behind 2-0 to Warriors in Ugly Loss

The Cleveland Cavaliers were thoroughly embarrassed by the Golden State Warriors in Game 2 of the NBA Finals. In response to a 15-point Warriors beat-down to open the series, Draymond Green and company used a savage display of basketball superiority to eliminate all hope of a bounce-back victory.

As the city of Cleveland watched in collective horror, Golden State bullied their way to a 46-34 advantage on the glass while passing the Cavaliers' defense into oblivion with 26 assists as a team. Despite resting for the final period, Green finished with a game-high 28 points as Stephen Curry and Klay Thompson added 18 and 17, respectively. LeBron James paced his squad with 19 and no other Cavalier scored more than 12 in a 110-77 blowout that left most observers thinking sweep.

The lone highlight for Cleveland came with 10:12 remaining in the second quarter. Matthew Dellavedova found James streaking through the middle of the paint for a high-flying finish that gave the Cavaliers a 28-22 momentary advantage. But before the Cavs fans huddled around their flat screens had a chance to put two hands together in celebration, the Warriors opened the heavy artillery. A deep three from Thompson sparked a 7-0 run that gave Golden State a 29-28 lead 71 seconds later. They'd go on to dismantle a lifeless Cleveland team by winning the third quarter by 12 points and the fourth by 13, before securing a 33-point victory on the game's biggest stage. The loss would send LeBron and the Cavaliers back to Northeast Ohio searching for answers as headlines proclaiming their demise littered the internet.

"We didn't play hard," Tristan Thompson admitted following the Bay Area massacre. "They won the 50-50 balls, they wanted it more than us tonight and it shows in the outcome."

The Warriors' desire to take care of business also showed in every major statistical category. They shot a better percentage from three-point range (46%) than the Cavaliers did from the floor as a team (35.4%) while knocking down 15 triples compared to only five for Cleveland.

Golden State also forced James and Kyrie Irving to combine for 10 turnovers, as Irving struggled mightily to understand and attack the Warriors' switching defense. The point guard Nike once signed to a signature shoe deal over Curry finished 5-of-14 from the floor for a game-worst plus-minus rating of minus-26. J.R. Smith continued to be a non-factor for the second-straight night, and after scoring only five points in 21 minutes, Kevin Love's game was cut short by a concussion.

"I'm not disappointed in our guys or frustrated," James said defiantly from the podium following the embarrassing loss. "We've just got to do a better job. We've got to be better at all facets of the game both offensively and defensively, both physically and mentally."

It was the perceived mental approach the Cavaliers demonstrated throughout the lackluster performance that left fans and analysts wondering if it was even possible for Cleveland to upend a team that had now beaten them seven straight times dating back to last year's NBA Finals, even once in the series. Trailing

On the Cavaliers' bench (second from left to right) Kyrie Irving, LeBron James, J.R. Smith and teammates look on during the second half of Game 2. The Cavs lost the first two games of the series by a combined 48 points.

the team with the best regular-season record in NBA history 2-0—by a combined margin of 48 points—seemed thoroughly insurmountable. Nevertheless, the Cavs still had an opportunity to even the series at home if they could somehow make the right adjustments.

"Just going out there and when we have opportunities in transition and in the paint, finishing them better," Irving suggested as how the tide could be turned in Game 3. "Also attacking early, willing ourselves to understand that it will take a full 48 minutes to beat these guys. We start out the first quarter great, on the defensive end we're feeling good. We just have to keep consistency on both ends of the court and up our physicality."

Directly following a 12-of-36 combined effort over the first two games of the NBA Finals for Irving, significant adjustments seemed unlikely. But all Cleveland has ever had is hope, and Tyronn Lue reiterated that reason to believe in the wake of its destruction.

"We know going back home we have to play better," Lue said of the two home games that stood between his team and possible elimination. "And I'm sure we will play better." ∎

NBA FINALS

GAME 3: CAVALIERS 120, WARRIORS 90

June 8, 2016 · Cleveland, Ohio

NEW LIFE IN CLEVELAND

Cavs Strike Early and Often to Close Series Gap to 2-1

It was a tale of two cities as the 2016 NBA Finals shifted to Quicken Loans Arena. What was the worst of times for the Cavaliers in Oakland, quickly became the best of times as they returned to Cleveland for Game 3. Kyrie Irving signaled his difference-making arrival on basketball's biggest stage with a dazzling performance right from the tip, offering 16 points on 7-of-9 shooting in the opening period. LeBron James knocked down his first four shots of the contest, Richard Jefferson, J.R. Smith and Tristan Thompson each got on the board early as well, and the Cavaliers built a 20-point first-quarter lead that they'd eventually ride to a dominating victory over the Golden State Warriors, 120-90.

Starting in place of an injured Kevin Love—who was sidelined with a concussion suffered in Game 2—the 35-year-old Jefferson provided energy and spacing the Cavaliers desperately lacked in each of the previous matchups. He knocked down a three-pointer off an assist from Irving that gave his team a 9-0 lead in the opening minutes, before finishing with nine points and eight rebounds on the night to pair with solid work defensively.

James (game-high 32 points) and Irving (30 points) combined to score 62 on 26-of-51 shooting,

proving to be far and away the two best players on a court that included Stephen Curry, Klay Thompson and Draymond Green. J.R. Smith broke through a two-game shooting slump to hit five triples on his way to 20 points and Tristan Thompson double-doubled as the Cavs locked in at both ends of the floor to secure a win they desperately needed.

"We just talked about our 1-4 in pick-and-roll with me and (LeBron), with us leading our guys offensively," Irving said of his approach entering Game 3. "I know that I can't play in between or be indecisive, especially with guys in front of me. Just constantly in attack mode. I know my teammates consistently want me to do that, possession by possession, whether it's getting downhill or shooting jump shots or whatever it is."

As the Cavaliers broke through offensively, they also cleaned up their mental errors and blown assignments defensively to hold Curry to only two points in the first half. He and Thompson connected on only 4 of 16 three-pointers for the game, finishing 10-of-26 overall for 29 points combined. While matched up with Green—who had been primarily covered by Love during Games 1 and 2—James helped hold the Warriors' All-NBA forward to only six points on eight shots. Shaun Livingston and a Golden State

Tristan Thompson gets the shot up with Shaun Livingston, top, and Draymond Green, bottom, defending. Thompson had a strong game with 14 points and 13 rebounds.

bench that devastated Cleveland earlier in the series was similarly held in check, as the Cavs came out prepared for the fight of their lives while trailing a 73-win Warriors team 2-0 in the NBA Finals.

"I just think it's two words, physicality and aggressiveness," Lue said of his team's improved performance in Game 3. "I thought we were very physical defensively, and I thought we were aggressive offensively, attacking the basket, getting out in transition, running the floor. We talked about it before, that opens up shots for J.R. Smith and those guys in transition. So that's how we have to play."

The seminal moment for the Cavaliers in Game 3 came during the third quarter. While looking to build on an eight-point halftime lead, James used that physicality to dive for a loose ball near midcourt. He scrambled to his feet, found the handle, and quickly zipped a pass to his running mate Irving, who promptly accelerated down the left side of the court. The young point guard left a high lob pass up near the basket that only a few athletes in the history of civilization would ever be gifted enough to collect. During the gravity-defying sequence that followed, the Akron prodigy met the basketball that dangled out past the backboard with his right hand. He slammed home a finish with the aggression of a team that refused to die, announcing Cleveland's rebirth in a series that had only just begun.

"You have to be able to have a short mind, but also learn from the mistakes that you made the previous game and just try to better yourself in the following game," James said after Game 3. "And that's what we're able to do. Coach Lue and the coaching staff gave us a great game plan and it was just up to us to go out and execute that, and I think we did that tonight." ■

Richard Jefferson tries to contain Steph Curry during the Cavs' Game 3 win. Jefferson started for an injured Kevin Love and contributed nine points and eight rebounds.

NBA FINALS

GAME 4: WARRIORS 108, CAVALIERS 97
June 10, 2016 · Cleveland, Ohio

RUDE AWAKENING

Cavs Lose at Home, On the Brink of Elimination

The crippling pain of being seemingly eliminated in the 2016 NBA Finals after dropping the first two games by a combined total of 48 points was quickly replaced by a renewed optimism as the city of Cleveland flooded its downtown streets in anticipation of a pivotal Game 4. But the rising tide of hope and promise that emerged in the wake of a 30-point victory in Game 3 was sunk to new lows by a 38-point effort from league MVP Stephen Curry that left the city and its team with an insurmountable deficit—again. Curry's All-NBA performance was aided by 25 points from fellow Splash Brother, Klay Thompson, and the Golden State Warriors used a 108-97 decision to create a 3-1 series lead over the Cleveland Cavaliers.

"My mindset is get one," LeBron James said following the Game 4 loss at Quicken Loans Arena. "You know, we've got to go out there and play obviously better than we played tonight. Better than even we played in Game 3. But we've got to get one. It's not about overlooking this. It's about getting one on their home floor where they've been very successful. So, you know, we've got to come in with the mindset that our coaching staff is going to give us a great game plan and we've got to execute that. We're about the results after."

James turned in a 25-point, 13-rebound and nine assist effort in response to the Splash Brothers' brilliance, but the seven turnovers he gave away on the night were costly. Tristan Thompson kept the Cavaliers in the game during the first half with five offensive

rebounds in the opening quarter, and Kyrie Irving added a scoring punch that against most teams would've been enough for James to carry his Cavs to victory. Irving finished with 34 points and four assists, but no other Cavalier totaled more than 11 as he and James combined to attempt 33 of Cleveland's 38 shots in the second half.

"I'm following this guy to my right's lead," Irving said of his offensive production over the last two games following the loss. "Game 3 and 4 I've been put in positions to be successful and our guys have trusted me to be aggressive, whether that be in transition or in the half court. Our one-four pick-and-roll with LeBron playing the four has been working for us great. So we just have to be better in Game 5, and come in with the mindset to be aggressive for however many minutes we, myself and everyone else needs to play."

Kevin Love returned from a concussion to log all of his minutes off the bench in Game 4. His impact was minimal, however, totaling 11 points and five rebounds in his first NBA game as a reserve in six years. Starting in Love's place during Game 4 was Richard Jefferson who was similarly ineffective with three points and six rebounds in 25 minutes. After dominating the glass to begin the game, Thompson tired and collected only seven boards on the night along with totaling 10 points. J.R. Smith added 10 points as well, but it was far from enough as the Cavaliers boarded a plane back to the Bay with their backs to the wall.

"Yeah, I felt it was the right way to go," Lue said

Warriors big man Anderson Varejao, center, grabs a rebound ahead of Cleveland's LeBron James, Kevin Love and J.R. Smith, from left, during the second half in Game 4. The Warriors took a 3-1 series lead with the win.

after the game, when questioned about his decision to bring Love off the bench in favor of starting Jefferson. "We had just won a game by 30 points. We played well. So I just decided to stick with RJ. Kevin came to me after the game and just said, whatever I felt was right, coming off the bench or starting, he was all in. So after winning the game by 30 points, I thought it was the right thing to do."

Right or wrong, Love didn't perform in the biggest game of his career to date, and criticisms surrounding his fit, drive and ability would reach unprecedented heights over the next two days. Cleveland would get a break, however, after the league office reviewed a skirmish between James and Draymond Green with two minutes remaining in the contest. The Cavaliers suggested the play should've been called a Flagrant 2 on the floor, putting Green's eligibility in jeopardy for Game 5 in Oakland, and that's exactly what would happen, as he garnered a critical one-game suspension. ∎

NBA FINALS

GAME 5: CAVALIERS 112, WARRIORS 97

June 13, 2016 · Oakland, California

THE KYRIE & LEBRON SHOW

Superstar Duo Steps Up and Brings Series Back to Cleveland

LeBron James has never been measured by the metrics of traditional success. Like the transcendent figures before him known simply as Wilt, Oscar, Kareem, Larry, Magic, Michael and Kobe, LeBron's effort on the game's biggest stage has only ever been viewed through the lens of historical greatness. During the first four games of the 2016 NBA Finals, the Cavaliers' transcendent star had posted numbers that would qualify as traditionally good. But in order for Cleveland to become the first team in NBA history to emerge from a 3-1 deficit to dethrone the Golden State Warriors, an historic effort from James was required.

Following an incident in Game 4 which eventually led to a flagrant foul being assessed on Draymond Green—and a subsequent suspension for a collection of shots to the groin throughout the postseason—an uproar of criticism directed at James emerged from the Golden State camp. In ways that no opponent would ever dare to publicly speak of Bird, Jordan or Bryant in the midst of an NBA Finals Series, Klay Thompson, Marreese Speights, and others with Warrior affiliations directly questioned LeBron's manhood. But after allowing a close-out opportunity in front of their hometown crowd slip away at the conclusion of a 112-97 Cavs victory, it would be the city by the Bay who left with their feelings hurt.

"I think from a mental standpoint it wasn't about anybody that was on the floor," James said after sending a 3-2 series back to Cleveland for Game 6. "We just had a mindset that we wanted to come in here and just try to extend and have another opportunity to fight for another day. And that was our main concern, and we were able to do that."

James combined with Kyrie Irving to dominate all phases of the game. He finished with 41 points, 16 rebounds, and seven assists on a night where he excelled from all over the floor. As the Warriors continued to go under screens in defense of James— daring him to beat them from the outside—he found the range he lacked earlier on in the series while mixing in three-point buckets with hard drives to the rim. He also ignited the defensive attack in the second half, finishing with three steals and three monster blocks as the Cavaliers weathered a 26-point first half from Thompson to outlast the Warriors on the road for the first time all season.

In support of LeBron's heroics, Irving delivered the best performance of his NBA career when his team needed it most. The young point guard banked in

Kyrie Irving had a masterful performance in Cleveland's Game 5 win, converting on an incredibly efficient 17 of 24 shots for 41 points.

layups from all angles and knocked down a collection of turnaround jumpers and long-range triples in a display of genuine brilliance. He'd finish with 41 points on the night as well, marking the first time in NBA Finals history that two teammates exceeded the 40-point mark in the same game. James would later refer to Irving's magical effort as "probably one of the greatest performances I've ever seen live."

"Just sticking with our game plan and going off the trust of my teammates," Irving replied postgame to a question about how he was able to sustain his all-time great performance for 48 minutes. "We also got a lot of opportunities in transition that we weren't necessarily taking advantage of in Game 4, whether — for whatever reason. But I think as well is the way we spaced out our lineups and when guys were coming in, relieving us and giving us a few minutes here and there, it gave us an incredible amount of energy that we needed to sustain the high level that we were playing at."

Playing without one of the best all-around defenders in the NBA, that spacing was certainly aided by the suspension of Green. The Cavaliers' chances around the rim also increased due to an unfortunate injury suffered by Warriors big man Andrew Bogut, who appeared to be an intimidating presence around the basket throughout the series. If the Cavaliers were going to make history over the next two games, however, they would need two more elite performances from James and Irving no matter who they lined up against—which is exactly what Tyronn Lue expected as he boarded the plane back to Cleveland.

"Same thing," Lue added, when asked about what would be required of his team in Game 6. "Continue to be aggressive, continue to bring physicality and continue to attack." ■

LeBron James glides in for the finish as the Warriors look on helplessly. LeBron had a huge game with 41 points, 16 rebounds, and seven assists.

NBA FINALS

GAME 6: CAVALIERS 115, WARRIORS 101
June 16, 2016 • Cleveland, Ohio

KING JAMES SENDS IT BACK TO OAKLAND

LeBron Masterful Once Again as Cavs Force Game 7

Ernest Hemmingway once said the best way to find out if you can trust somebody is to trust them. Heading into Game 6 of the NBA Finals, Northeast Ohio had invested all of its trust in LeBron James to accomplish the impossible and he once again delivered.

Trailing the Golden State Warriors 3-2, James, in turn, trusted his teammates and coaches on the brink of elimination while removing any doubt that he was still the greatest basketball player on planet Earth. The totality of his performance—considering time, circumstance and overall brilliance—would require the eloquence of Hemmingway to accurately depict. The rest of us mere mortals were simply lost for words.

"I give a lot of credit to my teammates and my coaching staff to put me in position to be successful," James offered humbly in response to the two best games he ever played back to back in his NBA career. "I mean, without the ball moving, without the screens being set, without the coaching staff putting out the game plans for us offensively then, what I've been able to do, it doesn't happen. So those guys definitely get the credit."

The game plan that Tyronn Lue employed on the offensive end to help facilitate the 115-101 Cleveland Cavaliers victory was a dedication to using the Warriors' switching attack defensively against them. With more regularity than previously in the series, the Cavaliers screened Andre Iguodala off James with a teammate who was guarded by a Golden State defender they preferred to matchup with the King. Once Igoudala switched onto that screener, and James sized up the mismatch Cleveland had identified, the Cavs created the space necessary for James to attack the rim with ferociousness and frequency. He knocked down three triples to keep the defense honest, while converting 12 of his 16 field goals in the paint to score 41 points for the second straight game, along with dishing out 11 assists.

"It's LeBron being LeBron," Lue said following the superstar performance that also included eight rebounds and three momentum-changing blocks from James to go along with a 59 percent shooting effort

LeBron throws it down with force during the second half of Game 6 in Cleveland. LeBron had 41 points for the second consecutive game and further stated his Finals MVP case.

from the field. "He's one of the greatest of all-time. Our back was against the wall and he took it upon himself, him and Kyrie, they put us on their backs. They've got us to where we wanted to be—and that's Game 7. I thought we did a great job, just continued to attack in transition, in the half court, and make them guard us."

Alongside a dominating performance from the player that J.R. Smith publicly suggested was the real MVP of the NBA heading into the Finals matchup with two-time winner Stephen Curry, LeBron's teammates made the Warriors guard them as well. Kyrie Irving added 23 points, Smith chipped in 14 and Tristan Thompson offered the best game of his professional career by making all six of his field goals to score 15 points while collecting 16 rebounds and finishing with a game-high plus/minus rating of +32 in 43 minutes of meticulous work.

"Like LeBron and Kyrie said, be a star in your role," Thompson said from the halls of Quicken Loans Arena following the biggest win in franchise history. "Be a star in your role, and for me that's high energy, use my motor, just play hard. Play hard be relentless on the glass. And that's what I bring to this team. That's my job, just be a star in your role, and I try to do that every night."

The Warriors were playing without starting center Andrew Bogut who suffered a season-ending injury during Game 5. While only averaging 15 minutes per night in the series, Bogut had been a formidable presence at the rim, accounting for 10 blocked shots and changing direction on multiple Cleveland attempts.

While they were aided by the return from suspension of Draymond Green, the Golden State forward scored only eight points on 3-of-7 shooting. A frustrated Curry fired his mouthpiece into the stands after being ejected with 4:22 remaining for his sixth personal foul, striking a fan with the saliva-coated rubber projectile. But while Steph finished with 30 and Klay Thompson added 25, the three other Warrior starters combined for only 13 points as Harrison Barnes was blanked on 0-of-8 shooting.

"Yeah, I like our chances," Smith said of the trust he had for his Cavaliers teammates heading into Game 7. "If we keep playing the way we're playing now, I like our chances." ■

LeBron James blocks Steph Curry's shot, one of three blocks on the game for LeBron. Curry may have won the regular season MVP but LeBron had the superior NBA Finals.

NBA FINALS

GAME 7: CAVALIERS 93, WARRIORS 89
June 19, 2016 • Oakland, California

CROWNED

LeBron, Kyrie, and the Cavs End the Curse, Bring Title to The Land

"Cleveland! This is for you!"

The simple words of LeBron James that boomed through the national airwaves following Game 7 of the NBA Finals met the masses gathered in his city's streets with the grace of Shakespearean prose. James had defined his wonder of will on basketball's biggest stage, and delivered on a promise to rise above 52 years of defeat with one glorious victory. From Calvary Cemetery in Cleveland to Akron General Hospital, the spirit of every soul ever born to the The Land of Northeast Ohio smiled proudly on its favorite son. On June 19, 2016, the kid from Akron had made them all champions.

"I'm coming home with what I said I was going to do," LeBron James said after helping his Cavaliers become the first team to rally from a 3-1 series deficit to win the NBA Finals. "I can't wait to get off that plane, hold that trophy up and see all our fans at the terminal."

James capped off an MVP performance in the NBA Finals with a 27-point, 11-assist, and 11-rebound triple-double. He played all but one of the 48 minutes required to decide the greatest Game 7 in NBA history. As the final buzzer signaled an end to the 93-89 battle, Tyronn Lue sobbed on the Cleveland Cavaliers bench while James collapsed to the very

hardwood he had just conquered. His team had defeated a collection of Warriors from Golden State who very much deserved the title they bravely fought to defend. On this night, however, Cleveland was king, and its city would rejoice forever.

"It's not even a relief, it's excitement for us — as a team, as a franchise, as a city, as a community," LeBron said. "To be able to continue to build up our city, continue to be an inspiration to our city, it means everything and I'm happy to be a part of it."

With 53 seconds remaining, Kyrie Irving rose up to hit the biggest shot in Cavs franchise history when he connected on a 25-foot three-pointer with Stephen Curry defending to provide his team with a 92-89 advantage. The heroic dagger from the Cavaliers' point guard who suffered a season-ending injury on the same court 12 months earlier gave Irving his 26th point of the contest.

"I was just thinking that the next team that scores has a great chance of winning that championship, and I hope we can be the team that's on that end," Irving said about his go-ahead three-pointer.

It was the second triple he buried on the night, to go along with six rebounds, bettering the 17 points totaled by the two-time MVP he started opposite. He'd

LeBron James raises back a thunderous dunk while the Warriors' Klay Thompson trails. LeBron followed up his back-to-back 41-point performances with a masterful triple-double — 27 points, 11 rebounds, and 11 assists.

finish the series with averages of 27 points, four rebounds, and four assists on over 40 percent shooting from beyond the arc. If not for his superstar teammate, it was an effort worthy of the trophy bearing Bill Russell's name.

It's a fools-errand to attempt to describe what LeBron James actually did throughout the 2016 NBA Finals—especially during Games 5, 6, and 7. We all witnessed it. We all saw it. He gave us all the unforgettable emotions that raced through our veins as we watched. James turned professional sports into a fairy tale as he furiously chased a championship he promised to deliver. He gave children and adults alike all reason to hope, and all reason to dream. He played like the Chosen One, he led like the King, and he continued to make his case as one of the very best to ever play the game he so very much loves.

If history requires numbers to quantify his brilliance, LeBron offered 29.7 points, 11.3 rebounds, and 8.9 assists throughout the series to earn the Finals MVP. He poured his heart on the floor for 42 minutes per night, smashing chase-down blocks off the backboard that seemed to shatter both the glass and spirit of his championship-caliber opponent.

Standing in the crossroads of defeat, trailing the 73-win Warriors 3-1, James made the wish of a Cleveland resurgence appear more real with every shot he fired. He relentlessly pursued a dream his city so desperately shared, and inspired his teammates to continue the fight in the face of adversity. James would believe in Kevin Love even when others suggested he shouldn't, and the All-Star forward delivered in the deciding moment by collecting 14 rebounds and finishing with a game-high plus/minus rating of +19 in Game 7.

LeBron implored J.R. Smith to keep shooting, Iman Shumpert to keep defending, Tristan Thompson to keep scrapping, and they all showed up alongside their leader. More than he did it for legacy and legend, LeBron did it for them, and he did for us, reminding all who witnessed his finest achievement that victory is always within reach for those who dare to believe.

LeBron played 47 of a possible 48 minutes in Game 7, willing his team to a championship and winning the Finals MVP in the process.

Akron's own LeBron James brought a long-awaited championship back to the people of Cleveland and Northeast Ohio. It was a journey a lifetime in the making and one of the most unforgettable Game 7s in NBA history.

REGULAR SEASON

PROPERTY OF
BROWNS

Make Lerner
Notice the
FANS.

A MOMENT 52 YEARS IN THE MAKING

Cleveland Celebrates the End of the Drought, and the Journey to Get There

The video montages and uninspired documentaries had become as clichéd as the banal barbs over the last several decades. The narrative was both tired and numbing, missing the very essence of the story it failed to depict. It was certainly true that every person under the age of 52 had never witnessed a professional sports championship in the city of Cleveland. It was also true, on a handful of occasions, that this same city nestled proudly along the shores of Lake Erie came close enough to taste the champagne of victory without ever taking a sip. But what was often lost on the tale told through the tears of missed opportunity, was the unbreakable spirit that truly defined a community all along.

For five decades, mothers and fathers, aunts and uncles, grandparents, coaches and teachers passed along a tradition of hope and support inspired by a dream of sharing at least one collective moment in celebration of a championship that would last forever. For most who called Northeast Ohio home, it was never really about the Browns, the Indians, or the Cavaliers. For the people of Cleveland and Akron, Westlake and Eastlake, Strongsville and Mentor, Lakewood and Euclid, and everywhere else in between,

it was always about much more than that. The dream of winning a championship was about family and neighborhoods. It was about fathers kissing their daughters, mothers hugging their sons, and sharing a smile together on that day we all finally won.

The drive led by John Elway, pitch left up in the zone by Jose Mesa, and shot buried by Michael Jordan never defined the community of Northeast Ohio. In truth, these moments, and others like them, only ever combined to make that belief, hope and pride stronger. In the wake of sports' trivial versions of the word tragedy, the tradition of hope and resolve continued to be passed down through generations.

The Munilot remained full at all hours of the morning. The playoff games remained packed at Progressive Field. The sellouts continued at the Q even after The Decision. To assume that unbreakable spirit didn't have an impact in lifting the Cleveland Cavaliers from the depths of a 3-1 series deficit over the team with the greatest regular-season record in NBA history would be a mistake.

It would also be a mistake to underestimate the mental strength required from a person who grew up in the Northeast Ohio community to carry the burden

The Cleveland Browns won the city's last championship back in 1964 but have suffered through many lean years and a franchise relocation in the time since.

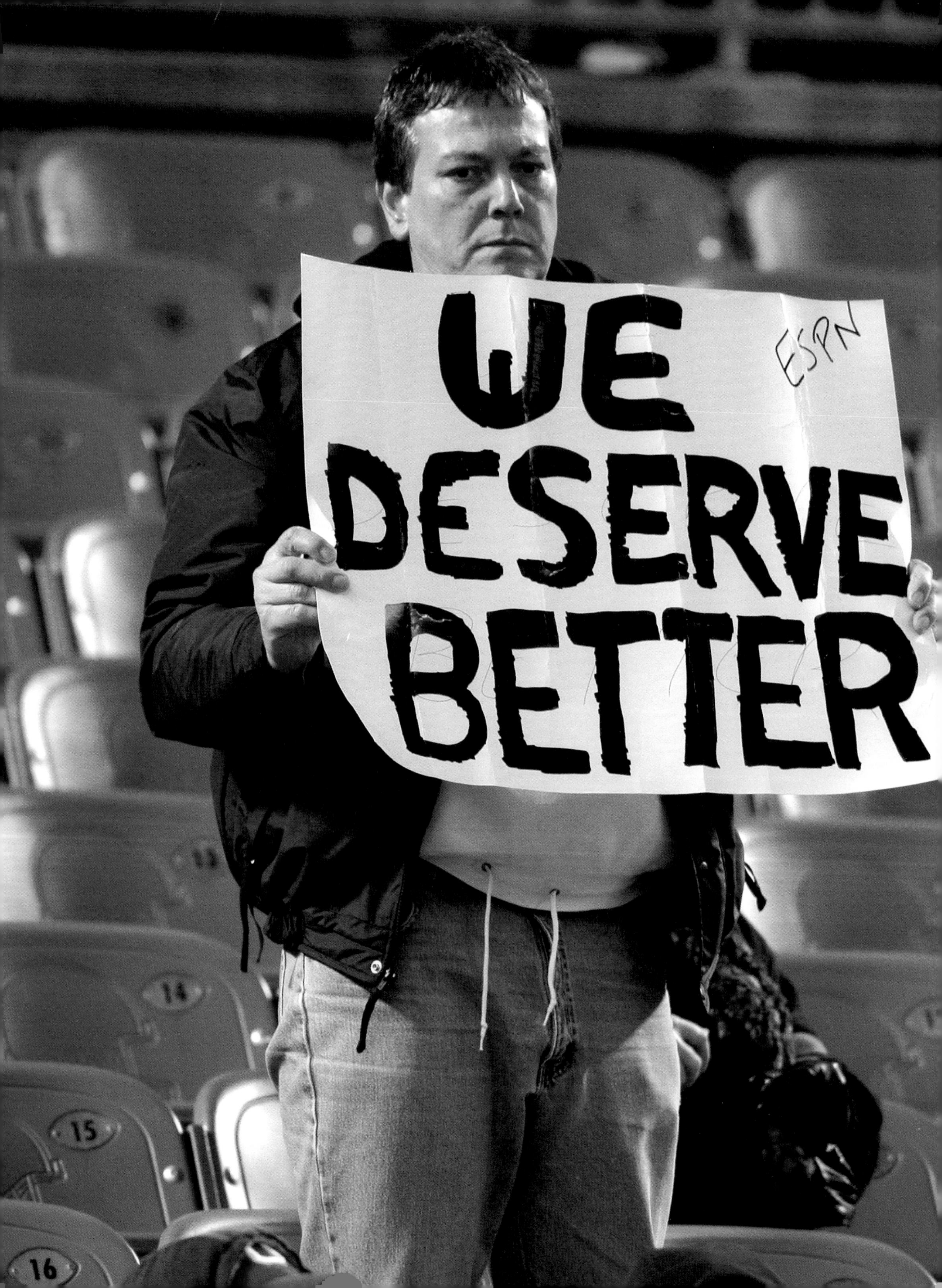
WE
DESERVE
BETTER
ESPN

of delivering this moment on his shoulders. LeBron James isn't from New Jersey, or Alabama, or Canada or Australia. He's from Akron, Ohio, a 40-minute drive from Quicken Loans Arena. He went to high school with our co-workers, played AAU with our friends, and always understood it would be up to him to secure his hometown its first championship since 1964. He may have left six years ago to momentarily escape that burden, but he'd eventually return and allow his legacy to be defined by his ability to accomplish something that had never happened in the history of his franchise. And just when it seemed as elusive as ever, the kid they called Bron Bron claimed a crown for a city it was always destined to wear.

LeBron and his Cavaliers wrote the final chapter in a Cleveland sports story that was 52 years in the making. He delivered a championship moment in Northeast Ohio not only for the fans of his professional sports team, but also his friends, relatives and neighbors—the very people who always knew he was the chosen one well before *Sports Illustrated* announced as much to the world. The 2016 Cleveland Cavaliers have afforded their community the same opportunity that Bob Feller's Indians did in 1948, and the Jim Brown-led Cleveland Browns last did in 1964. At this moment, Cleveland is king, as the land of champions who always believed can rejoice once more together. ∎

Cleveland sports fans are known for their passion and loyalty but both traits have been tested many times in the past 52 years.

Michael Jordan and the Bulls tormented Cleveland fans over the years, knocking Craig Ehlo and the Cavs out of the playoffs four times between 1988 and 1993, and a fifth time in 1994 during Jordan's first retirement.

Jose Mesa's blown save in Game 7 of the 1997 World Series against the Florida Marlins is one of the most infamous moments in Cleveland sports history. Cases of champagne and the World Series trophy were wheeled into, then out of the Indians clubhouse when Mesa blew the save, ultimately costing the Indians a championship.

ONE GOAL

Cavs Emerge from Eventful Regular Season with Title or Bust Aspirations

The Cleveland Cavaliers' journey through the 2015-16 regular season was hardly a trumpeted march toward inevitable glory. While it was certainly promising at times to be sure, for fans on board for the ride it often felt more like a dead-end than it did a road to Cleveland's first title in 52 years. But in a season of comebacks, dismissals, adversity, drama and triumph, it was those same valleys that helped this collection of Cavaliers develop the championship mettle required to peak at just the right time. All of which began in earnest during a 97-95 loss to the Chicago Bulls that was followed by the first win of the year on October 28.

LeBron James Declares Kevin Love the Focal Point

Playing without Kyrie Irving and Iman Shumpert, an undermanned Cavs team bounced back from a two-point loss in Chicago to earn its first victory of the season during a 106-75 decision over the Memphis Grizzlies on Beale Street. The win snapped a four-game losing streak dating back to Game 4 of the 2015 NBA Finals, and signaled the healthy return of Kevin Love. Playing opposite Marc Gasol and Zach Randolph, Love finished with 17 points and 13 rebounds in his second game back from a season-ending shoulder injury suffered six months earlier.

"We'll use Kevin however he wants to be used," James announced to the media following the game in Memphis. "I told you Kevin is going to be our main focus. He's going to have a hell of a season. He's going to get back to that All-Star status. He's the focal point of us offensively. I know I can go out and get mine when I need it. But I need Kev to be as aggressive as he was tonight, and when he rebounds at the level he did tonight, the shots will automatically fall for him."

Love was every bit as aggressive as James needed him to be during his first two games back from injury. He totaled 35 points against Chicago and Memphis in support of 37 from LeBron, averaging 17.5 points, 10.5 rebounds and 3.5 assists to begin the season. He'd also close out the month of November averaging 20 points and 12 rebounds while appearing to be on his way to the All-Star appearance James suggested. But that production, along with his role as the focal point of the Cavaliers attack offensively, would be challenged significantly upon Irving's return to the lineup in December.

Kyrie Irving Returns in Cleveland

On December 20, 2015, Kyrie Irving logged 17 minutes during a 108-86 victory over the Philadelphia 76ers. Despite the loss being welcomed by the tanking group from Philly, it more importantly marked the first appearance on an NBA court for Irving since suffering a broken kneecap in Game 1 of the Finals. Since June, Irving had rehabbed tirelessly to regain the electric first step he used to burst into the Association as the No. 1 overall pick in 2012, and the early returns were promising.

Life with LeBron James and the Cleveland Cavaliers is always eventful but the 2015-16 regular season stands out, as it set the table for the first championship in franchise history.

"Those are the steps that we need to take," Irving replied, when asked about the timeline for increasing his minutes over the next several weeks. "Obviously, the first game back, we weren't trying to push it too hard and I just wanted to go out there and see how it felt. Staying on the bike until my number was called and then just being ready to play. That is where I am right now and hopefully every game I continue to progress and feel better."

After missing his first five shots of the game, Irving connected on a layup off a pass from LeBron with 8:57 remaining in the second quarter for his first two points of the season. The bucket gave Cleveland a 29-27 lead that they'd never relinquish. He'd finish strong from there, connecting on four of his next seven field goals to total 12 points, four assists and two steals. Irving would go on to score 22 against the Phoenix Suns eight days later, and follow that up with 25 against the Toronto Raptors on January 4. His breakout night would come two days later, when he exploded for 32 against the Washington Wizards.

Warriors Return to Talk Champagne and Clown Cavs

Stephen Curry and the Golden State Warriors returned to Quicken Loans Arena on January 18 and promptly burned everything David Blatt and his Cavaliers thought they built directly to the ground. Playing against a Cavs team now at full strength, Curry scored 35 points on his way to a 132-98 victory that turned Dan Gilbert's franchise on its head. To say it was the lowest point of the regular season would be an understatement. LeBron James, Kyrie Irving and Kevin Love combined to total only 27 points in response, as Curry taunted Cleveland on his way out the door.

"Still smells a little bit like champagne," Curry said, in reference to the visitor's locker room he used to celebrate the Warriors' NBA Finals clinching victory the season before. "The last time I was there, we had a trophy, we had champagne and we had goggles. We had a good time."

The Warriors led by 30 points in the first half and as many as 43 before securing their fifth straight win over the Cavaliers. Blatt didn't know it at the time, but his tenure as the head coach in Cleveland ended for all intents and purposes as soon as the final buzzer offered a merciful

Kevin Love was able to add a championship to his résumé before fellow NBA star Kevin Durant.

reprieve to the dumpster fire.

"We had a breakdown and we didn't respond to it," Blatt said after the game. "That and the lack of mental preparation more than anything else really hurt us. I told my guys that it starts with me. If they're not mentally ready to play, I take responsibility for that. We never gave ourselves a chance to win that game and that's unfortunate and tough, and we have to live with that. We have to face up to that and use that as a new starting point to improve."

Four days later, on January 22, Blatt was fired after amassing a 30-11 record to begin the season.

The Tyronn Lue Era Opens in Defeat

Cleveland Cavaliers general manager David Griffin introduced Tyronn Lue as his new head coach during a press conference on January 22. The Cavs' highest paid assistant was now tasked with accomplishing the only thing the man before him was unable to do in his short time on the job—win an NBA Championship. Anything less for Griffin, Lue, LeBron James and the Cavaliers would be a total, complete and utter failure. That mission got off to a rocky start, however, as Lue's Cavaliers were booed off the court following a 106-93 loss to the Chicago Bulls the next day.

"I don't think we're in good enough shape," Lue said following his first game as head coach of the Cavaliers. "Early, we wanted to push it, we wanted to open the floor, and we came out and did that and then we just dropped off the map. We got tired. I just don't think we're in good enough shape right now to play in the style that we want to play."

The comment was not so much an indictment of Blatt as it was a declaration on how Lue believed his team could ultimately succeed. With the offensive firepower that James, Kevin Love and Kyrie Irving possessed, Lue's vision of the Cavaliers was a group that dictated offense to whoever they played on a nightly basis. It was a challenge that James appeared willing to embrace, too, in the wake of a coaching change he certainly didn't oppose.

"We have to get in better shape," James reiterated, after finishing with 26 points, 13 rebounds and nine assists in the 13-point loss. "Coach wants us to play faster, so we need to start doing stuff on off days, at practice and during

Head coach Tyronn Lue's tenure started slowly but ended with a historic and memorable NBA Finals comeback from a 3-1 deficit.

shoot around. We just have to get up and down the floor because he wants us to play at a faster pace than we have done in the past. We all need to get in better shape."

Cavs' Quickened Pace Beats Thunder by 23

Three weeks after a statement win on January 30 against the San Antonio Spurs, the Cavaliers continued to demonstrate an improved ability to compete with the best teams in the Western Conference. On the road, in a matchup with Kevin Durant and Russell Westbrook, the revamped Cavs defeated the Oklahoma City Thunder 115-92. The February 21 victory—against the best team in the West not named Golden State or San Antonio—helped build a renewed confidence in their quickened style that Cleveland would eventually ride into the Eastern Conference Playoffs.

"Offensively, you want to push the pace but that doesn't mean you have to take early shots," James explained following the victory. "You want to push the tempo. You want to get the ball up with 19 on the clock, which we did not tonight. We had shots and we took them. I think we did well on both sides, we were able to push tempo when we had it, were able to execute as well, and we were able to get back and defend."

Kevin Love emerged in a big spot for the Cavaliers to lead all scorers with 29 points and 11 rebounds while James added 25. Despite 26- and 20-point efforts from Durant and Westbrook, respectively, the Cavs bench outscored the OKC reserves 30-21 behind 15 points from Richard Jefferson. If a team is going to succeed at the pace Tyronn Lue wants to play, productive minutes and scoring off the bench is a necessity—and Cleveland was beginning to demonstrate that gear. They'd go on to close out the No. 1 seed in the East with a 17-11 mark following the win in Oklahoma City, believing they had plenty of answers for anybody they'd eventually face in the NBA Finals.

Subtweets, Snapchats, Lil Kev and Camaraderie

Before he entered "Zero Dark 23" mode, silencing his social media platforms for the postseason, LeBron James posted a series of comments to his Twitter account from March 1-5 that created questions about the Cavaliers' chemistry—

Some criticized the Cavs for signing Tristan Thompson, left, to a 5-year, $82 million contract prior to the season but he was an essential ingredient in their championship mix.

fair or not. Maybe the comments meant nothing at all, maybe he was trying to send a motivational message to his teammates, or maybe they meant that LeBron hated Kevin Love and Kyrie Irving and never wanted to talk with them ever again—the latter gaining the most steam amongst reality-show inspired fans thirsting for drama.

Whatever the case, posts like this…

"It's ok to know you've made a mistake. Cause we all do at times. Just be ready to live with whatever that comes with it and be with those who will protect you at all cost!"

This…

"Can't replace being around great friends that reciprocate the same energy back to you in all facets of life"

This…

"The ultimate level of chemistry is when you know what I'm thinking without saying a word and we execute it. Visa Versa. #TheDC #SFG"

And this…

"It's this simple. U can't accomplish the dream if everyone isn't dreaming the same thing everyday. Nightmares follow. #TheDC #SFG"

The posts didn't combine to suggest that all was well within the Cavaliers universe behind the scenes as the postseason approached.

But after the 35-year-old Richard Jefferson finally figured out how to use Snapchat, those rumors and suggestions would fade to the background. Jefferson's Snapchat account would rise to national prominence with the help of Lil Kev—a Flat Stanley like character who wore a Hawaiian Shirt that RJ believed to share a resemblance with Love. His videos with Lil Kev—seated in the front seat of his car as he picked Channing Frye up for practice— along with jokes on James, Love, Frye, Kyrie Irving and the rest of the Cavaliers demonstrated a much more unified locker room than those predicted in the wake of LeBron's twittering. Turns out, what fans saw through the lens of RJeff24 on Snap was much more indicative of who the Cavaliers really were, and they rode that collective bond of basketball brotherhood all the way to a championship. ■

Richard Jefferson brought expected veteran savvy and leadership to the Cavs but became an unlikely source for team bonding and chemistry with his Snapchat antics.

23

SMALL FORWARD

LEBRON JAMES

When Faced with Adversity, LeBron Chooses Greatness

In a small college gym located in Teaneck, New Jersey, the No. 1 overall player in America offered a series of crossover dribbles before pulling up to bury a midrange jumper during the early minutes of the first half. With the swagger of New York City dangling from his outstretched shooting hand, Lenny Cooke held his release as the crowd gathered inside the Adidas ABCD camp erupted in applause. The marquee event's defending MVP shuffled back down the court like a conquering hero, while his young defender from somewhere in Ohio dusted off a shot that had just dotted his eye.

At that moment, in July of 2001, a sixteen year old named LeBron James could've gone one of two ways. His opponent, Cooke, was the best prospect produced by the New York City playgrounds in over a decade. He was a superstar already; a can't-miss talent who was simply biding his time before the NBA came calling. James, meanwhile, was from the basketball equivalent of nowhere, representing a city named Akron known more for its tires than its talent. If he didn't beat the kid from New York that day, nobody would've blamed him. But a young LeBron refused to back down.

Over the next several minutes, James would put not only himself, but also his city on the national map for good. He'd respond to Cooke's early offense by eventually outscoring him 21-9 in an individual duel as the game entered its final possession. Trailing by two points, while being guarded by Cooke, LeBron emerged from the backcourt dribbling down the right side of the floor. He'd lift off from just beyond the three-point line, letting a shot go as the buzzer expired that found nothing but the bottom of the net. The long-range bomb would propel James past Cooke, and he'd return to Ohio with the title of best player in America for the very first time.

Thirteen July's later, when James returned from the Miami Heat to the Cleveland Cavaliers, he reminded the audience gathered outside an event celebrating his signing that he was still just a kid from Akron. Standing then, in 2014, as a corporate mega-brand worth billions, and arguably the most popular athlete in the world, it was hard for most observers to grasp the concept. When he added that he wasn't supposed to be here, we thought of a 6-8 frame and Einstein-level basketball IQ that inspired some to collectively

LeBron James had an unbelievable year on and off the court, as his lifetime contract with Nike was revealed to be worth more than $1 billion.

LeBron may not have won the MVP award for the 2015-2016 season but his numbers were exemplary once again – 25.3 points, 7.4 rebounds, and 6.8 assists per game.

snicker in response. But the truth is, Lenny Cooke was once where LeBron James wanted to be. And unlike the series of tragic mistakes that Cooke would make to derail a promising professional career before it ever started, James is the kid who did everything right.

Standing now in the wake of his greatest professional conquest, it's important we remember where it is that LeBron came from even if we believe we never forgot. Like Cooke, and thousands of other talented young prospects before him, James could've been a statistic. The son of a poor, single mother on welfare, he beat the odds. He not only identified people who had his best interest at heart, but he also listened and acted upon their advice. Instead of acquiring NBA fortunes only to waste it away on extravagance, he invested his earnings, put his team and community in a position to succeed, and is on his way to joining a class of billionaires upon retirement. And along that path to greatness, both on and off the floor, he accepted a challenge for the same community he first put on the national map at ABCD camp to deliver a moment of championship glory that had eluded the area for 52 years.

Down 3-1 to the Golden State Warriors, James dusted himself off from a series of jumpers that Stephen Curry and Klay Thompson used to dot his eye just like the best player in America once did 15 years earlier. At that moment, LeBron and his Cavaliers could've gone one of two ways. But when he got up, he'd deliver a basketball championship to a city that never experienced one before. LeBron James the person did that, as much as LeBron James the player, and we owe it to that kid from Akron to always remember as much. ∎

LeBron finally accomplished the one career accolade that previously eluded him in bringing a championship back to the city of Cleveland and Northeast Ohio.

At 31 years old LeBron is reaching what is traditionally the tail end of an NBA player's prime, but he's shown no signs of slowing down, still dominating the league on a nightly basis.

PLAYER PROFILE

2
POINT GUARD
KYRIE IRVING
Kyrie Overcomes Injuries and Doubters, Emerges with a Ring

Kyrie Irving pulled up in the nation's capital five feet beyond the arc with 1:45 remaining in a January 6 matchup with Washington Wizards. He let loose on a long-range jumper that climbed over the out-stretched hand of a defender before slicing through the net to give his Cleveland Cavaliers a 119-105 lead that they'd never relinquish. The three-point field goal capped off a 32-point effort from Irving in the wake of six-plus months of bone-rattling rehab.

After missing the first 24 games of the 2015-16 season due to a broken kneecap suffered in Game 1 of the NBA Finals—and two of the previous eight heading into Washington—the godson of Rod Strickland was still very much capable of making them jump.

"Coming into that fourth quarter, I just wanted to be aggressive, not only for myself but for my teammates," Irving said after the game. "They were hitting some tough shots, they got it going, cut down our lead. LeBron gets it going in the third quarter, he gets a bunch of threes and the game is still close. They continued to battle. I mean, their transition game is unbelievable, led by John Wall. They're getting it going no matter what, got some transition threes but we got timely stops in the fourth quarter."

Despite a series of untimely injuries, the No. 1 overall pick of the 2012 NBA Draft had proven to be one of the most unique talents in basketball by his fourth season in the league. He combined one of the best crossovers since Allen Iverson with a jump shot wet enough to change a game on a moment's notice to earn Rookie of the Year honors and multiple trips to the All-Star game.

At 6-3, the 24-year-old point guard's ability to also play the off-guard position blended well with LeBron James, helping to form one of the most dynamic one-two punches in the Association. But the true test for Irving—who LeBron would refer to as his team's quarterback—would inevitably be measured by wins and losses, along with his ability to inspire collective greatness from those around him.

The kid who once teamed with Michael Kidd-Gilchrist at St. Patrick's High School in New Jersey had already cashed in both on and off the court by his 24th birthday.

His starring role as Uncle Drew in a viral campaign for Pepsi coupled with the launch of his signature Nike shoe, and other lucrative endorsement deals, to help make Irving one of the biggest corporate brands in

Many doubted the ability of Kyrie Irving to adjust his game to sharing the stage with another superstar in LeBron James, but their cohesion was on full display during Game 5 of the Finals. They became the first teammates in Finals history to both score 40 points or more, each finishing with 41.

Kyrie Irving maneuvers the shot over Warriors center Anderson Varejao. Irving had a terrific NBA Finals run, including 30 points in Cleveland's Game 3 win.

the NBA. But as rival point guard Stephen Curry rose to dominance in the West, critics began to question Irving's durability and leadership while wondering aloud if his brand had become bigger than his actual game. Throughout the next six months that followed his therapeutic night in Washington, Irving would be under the microscope during a championship-or-bust mission for Cleveland.

Kyrie would pass all preliminary tests by closing the regular season with averages of 19.6 points and 4.7 assists. He'd also improve on his three-point field goal efficiency during the first three rounds of the playoffs—raising a career-low 32.1 percent in the regular season to well over 40 throughout the Cavs' postseason run through the East. He'd return to the NBA Finals both healthy and productive, averaging over 23 points and five assists.

But on the game's biggest stage, playing opposite the first unanimous MVP in NBA history, Irving would stumble again along his path to immortality. He shot 12-of-36 and finished with a combined plus/minus rating of minus-33 in the Cavaliers' two humiliating losses, before overcoming the biggest obstacle in his young but storied career.

"I know that I can't play in-between or be indecisive, especially with guys in front of me," Irving said, following a 30-point performance that fueled a 120-90 Game 3 victory that proved to be the turning point of the series. "Just constantly in attack mode. I know my teammates consistently want me to do that, possession by possession, whether it's getting downhill or shooting jump shots or whatever it is."

Irving remained in attack mode, playing downhill and elevating his team to greatness while securing a come-from-behind Finals win. The point guard for the Cavaliers would lead Cleveland to its first championship in 52 years when most critics expected retreat. He'd also prove durable and worthy, while making the Vine videos, endorsement deals, and individual accolades a mere footnote on a basketball résumé that now featured the game's greatest triumph. ■

After missing 24 games recovering from an injury to start the season, Kyrie rounded into top form in time for the NBA Finals, leading the Cavs to the first championship in franchise history.

Irving's early years with the Cavs were lean for the franchise, as the team went 78-152 over three seasons. In the two years since, they've won an NBA title, made the Finals twice, and won 110 regular season games.

0

POWER FORWARD

KEVIN LOVE

Love Adjusts to New Role with Cavs with Championship Results

Kevin Love was formally introduced as a member of the Cleveland Cavaliers on August 26, 2014. Two years earlier, he stood alongside LeBron James on a court in London with an American Flag draped across his shoulders and a gold medal dangling from his neck. Upon his return to Northeast Ohio, the first call James made was to his Olympic teammate, asking Love to join the fight in Cleveland. The All-Star power forward from the Minnesota Timberwolves would agree to a trade that finalized the union soon after.

The marriage between Love, James, Kyrie Irving and the Cavaliers would eventually deliver a championship less than 24 months after the inception of Cleveland's Big 3. But in order to maximize the collective talent of the triumvirate along the way, Love would be asked to make sacrifices most NBA players of his stature would never consider. He arrived in Cleveland as a three-time All-Star, All-NBA player and regarded by some as the best power forward in the game. For the Cavaliers to ultimately succeed as a team, however, Love would be forced to reinvent that all-world game entirely.

Love's ability and willingness to make the changes he did as an individual player and still perform at an elite level is the primary reason Cleveland's Big 3 was able to succeed as a unit. It's also something often overlooked when it comes to the narrative surrounding the supremely versatile Love. For six seasons in Minnesota Love—the player who was drafted as a 20-year-old center out of UCLA in 2008—averaged 19.2 points and 12.2 rebounds as the focal point of the franchise. Everything ran through Love offensively, and he always knew when and where his touches would come. He'd attempt 53.8 percent of his field goals from areas 10 feet away and in from the basket for the Timberwolves, with only 23.6 percent of his shots coming from three-point range. But the winning recipe in Cleveland required a different ingredient.

Besides his total field goal attempts going down alongside James and Irving, Love was also asked to primarily use his shot-making ability from the perimeter to open driving lanes for his teammates by dragging opposing bigs away from the basket. His paint touches decreased significantly as a result, as Love attempted 45 percent of his field goals from three-point range and only 36 percent from 10 feet and in for the Cavs by year two.

Kevin Love mixed an inside-outside offensive game to average 16 points on the season.

That transition wasn't always easy, especially on a team where the two primary ball handlers are also its two leading scorers. But as the 2015-16 campaign wore on, Love began to hit his stride at just the right time. He'd average 16 points and 9.9 rebounds during the regular season before turning in his best stretch of basketball as a Cavalier when his team and city needed it most.

Despite averaging 18.9 points and 12.5 rebounds during the first eight games of the postseason, however, Love's critics would never be louder than they were during the Eastern Conference Finals. In each of the Cavaliers' two losses to the Toronto Raptors, he struggled to score only 6.5 points per night while shooting a combined 21.7 percent from the floor. He was admittedly awful during those two games, but responded by averaging 22.5 points and seven rebounds in the next two on 61.9 percent shooting to help secure a berth in the NBA Finals. He'd then open Game 1 against the Golden State Warriors with 17 and 13 before helping Cleveland defeat a team with the best regular-season record in NBA history in dramatic fashion.

"I really just focused on getting on the glass," Love said, about stretches of the season when his scoring opportunities and numbers dipped. "Rebounding can be something constant for me even when I have an off shooting night."

As the Finals concluded, standing on a court alongside LeBron James once again—this time draped in the glow of an NBA championship—all the sacrifices Love made for his team had paid off. He had helped secure an elusive title that first appeared possible on the August day he arrived in Cleveland, while adding another chapter in a Hall of Fame career. ■

Love was much maligned at times during his second season with the Cavs but his consistency can't be overlooked. He started and played 77 of 82 games, and could be counted on for at least 16 points and 10 boards on most nights.

Love finished with over 700 rebounds for the sixth time in his career, pulling down 762 on the season and averaging 9.9 per game.

5

SHOOTING GUARD

J.R. SMITH

Smith's Gunslinger Approach a Perfect Fit for Cavs

Earl Joseph "J.R." Smith III was born to let it fly. As the shooting guard for the 2015-16 Cleveland Cavaliers, he flourished in a role that required him to be exactly himself. But it wasn't always this natural for the 12-year NBA veteran who entered the league directly out of St. Benedict's Prep in Newark, New Jersey.

After being named co-MVP alongside Dwight Howard of the 2004 McDonald's All-American Game, Smith was drafted with the 18th pick overall by the New Orleans Hornets. He'd make two more professional stops as a member of the Denver Nuggets and New York Knicks before finding a home that seemed crafted specifically for Smith by the basketball gods.

With a smile on his face, the player once labeled a locker room malcontent thrived in Cleveland as a teammate of LeBron James. He also graciously welcomed the directive from Coach Tyronn Lue to fire away at all costs. Whether he was falling down, had a hand in his face, or was stepping into an open look in transition, the Cavaliers needed Smith to be a consistent weapon from beyond the arc. During a game against the Milwaukee Bucks on April 5, he'd ceremoniously fulfill that mission by knocking down seven triples to set the Cavs' franchise record for most three-pointers made in a single season.

"I think it was the third one, honestly," Smith said while colorfully describing the moment he believed he caught fire during the 39-point win over the Bucks when he set the record. "When I shot it, I felt a little bit off-balanced but I just held my follow through and it kind of rimmed in. After that, it felt like all of them were going down."

Smith would finish the regular season shooting 40 percent from three while knocking down a record-setting 204 from deep. Those totals were also good for seventh in the NBA overall in three-pointers made and 21st in efficiency. But Smith was not simply a three-point specialist. At multiple times during the season, Coach Lue used his post game press conference to refer to Smith as "the best on-ball defender" on the team. But it was his brash delivery from three-point range that helped provide the biggest spark along the Cavaliers' run to immortality.

"Everybody keeps telling me to keep shooting,"

J.R. Smith's deadly long-range shooting and effervescent personality were essential during the Cavs' title run.

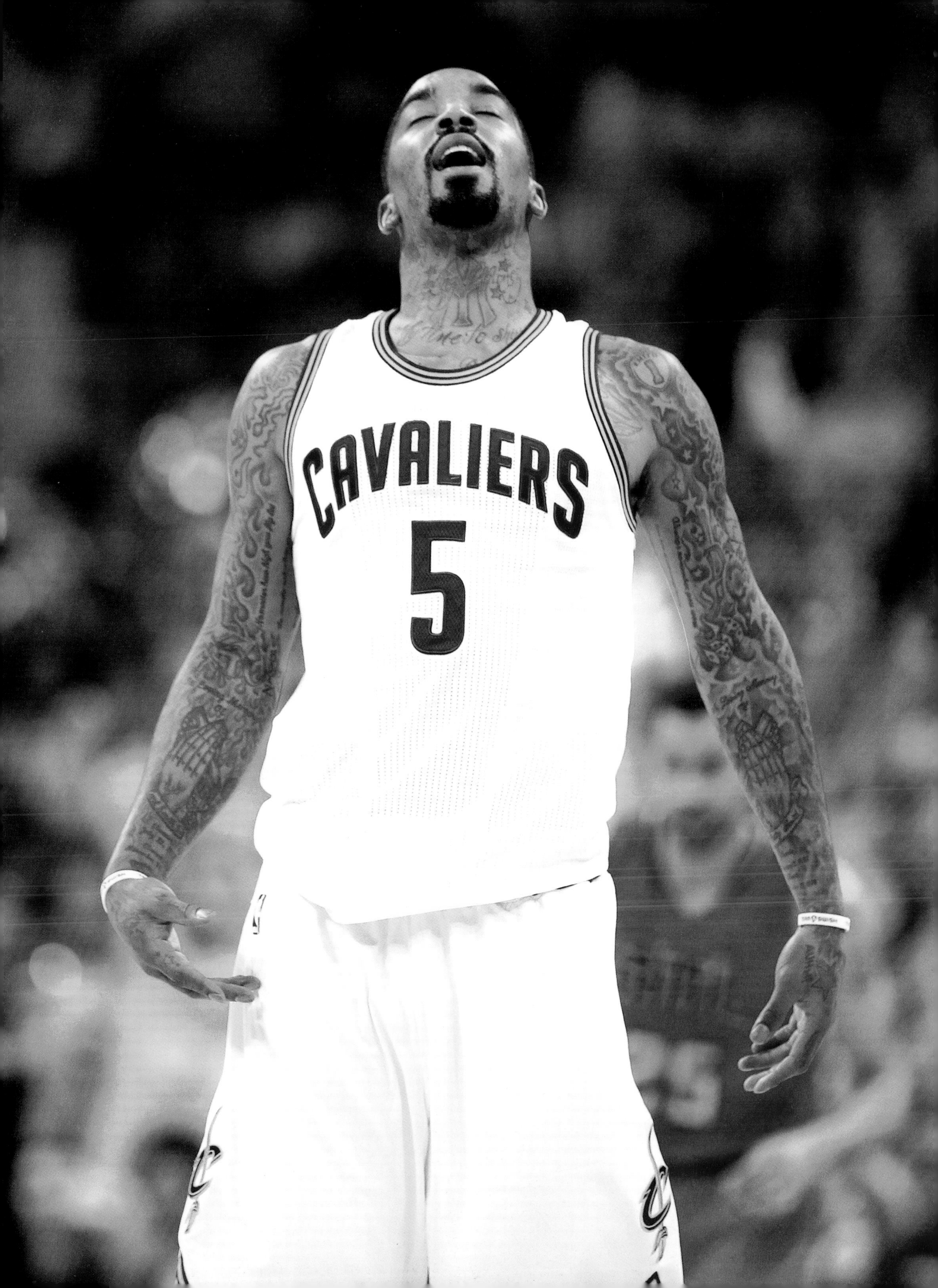
CAVALIERS
5

Smith said as the Cavaliers postseason run approached. "Everybody is enthused, especially the guys on the bench. I think we're feeding off a great energy coming into the playoffs and we're understanding who we are and what type of team we need to be. We're always looking to get better, I can't say we are there yet, but we're close. So we'll see what we can do."

During the Cavaliers' march to the NBA championship, it was more of the same from Smith as he offered a dizzying performance from deep on a routine basis. He hit seven three-pointers in Game 2 against the Detroit Pistons, and seven more in Game 2 against the Atlanta Hawks. Heading into the NBA Finals matchup with the Golden State Warriors, Smith had connected on 49 of 106 three-point field goals to lead the Cavaliers in that category through 14 games. He'd also improve his efficiency to a stifling 46 percent. The player who was initially perceived as a risky asset forced upon David Griffin in a trade with the Knicks for an opportunity to acquire Iman Shumpert had become the long-range assassin Cleveland needed to secure its first championship in 52 years.

"This is something that I would love to see because of my play style," Smith said following an Eastern Conference Semifinals game where the Cavaliers set an NBA record by knocking down 25 threes in a blowout victory. "But I think this is a credit of just how hard we work. We work on our shots every day and we are all very competitive with each other when it comes to shooting. I'm glad it happened."

Cavaliers fans will always be glad that this season happened exactly when it did for Smith, too. And in Cleveland, no matter how long his franchise three-point record may hold, the work put in by Earl Joseph "J.R." Smith III will never be forgotten. ■

Smith spends much of his time around the three-point line — knocking down 204 threes on the season — but can still finish with a flourish with the best of them.

13
CENTER
TRISTAN THOMPSON

Thompson's Heart, Hustle, and Energy Shine in Title Run

On February 10, 2012, a 20-year-old rookie from Toronto, Ontario collected 13 rebounds for the lottery-bound Cleveland Cavaliers during a 113-112 loss to the Milwaukee Bucks. Four games later, the fourth Canadian-born player to ever be named to the McDonald's All-American Game posted the first double-double of his NBA career with 15 and 12 during a 93-92 win over the Sacramento Kings. Nearly five years and more than 3,000 rebounds later, Tristan Thompson's heart, energy and production has remained more of a constant than anyone could've ever imagined when Chris Grant used a controversial selection to make the Texas Longhorn his fourth overall pick of the 2011 Draft.

Two weeks after his 25th birthday, Thompson posted the 113th double-double of his Cavaliers career while playing in his 362nd consecutive NBA game dating back to that night in early February of 2012. The appearance broke a franchise record set by the great Jim Chones that had stood for more than 40 years. He'd extend his streak of consistency and reliability to 370 straight appearances before his finest

hour as a professional athlete began on basketball's biggest stage. During Game 6 of the NBA Finals, the 6-9 forward proved both reliable and flawless when Cleveland needed him most. While setting a series of game-changing screens, Thompson made all six of his field-goal attempts, finishing with 16 points and 10 rebounds.

"For me, my approach is simple," Tristan Thompson once told *SLAM Magazine* of his role alongside LeBron James, Kyrie Irving and Kevin Love for the Cavaliers. "I call it, 'see ball, get ball'. I am going to put myself in a position on the court to rebound the basketball well for our team, then finish around the rim while also making an impact defensively."

Thompson matched a season high by collecting 16 boards during the 43 minutes of tireless execution that helped his Cavaliers force Game 7. He saw the ball, and used every ounce of his being to get the ball, grabbing 13 or more rebounds in each of Cleveland's first three Finals victories. His accomplishments may always be met with revisionist historians who remind us that Klay Thompson and Kawhi Leonard were still on the draft

Klay Thompson drives on Tristan Thompson during the Cavs' big Game 6 win in the 2016 NBA Finals. Tristan Thompson had a monster game, scoring 15 points on a perfect 6-of-6 shooting from the floor, and pulling down 16 rebounds.

board the night Tristan first became a Cavalier. But the only thing we now know is that the 2016 Cavs would not have won Cleveland its first championship in 52 years without the kid born just north of Lake Erie.

"Like LeBron and Kyrie said, be a star in your role," Thompson said following the victory that evened the NBA Finals at 3-3. "Be a star in your role, and for me that's high energy, use my motor, just play hard. Play hard, be relentless on the glass. And that's what I bring to this team. That's my job, just be a star in your role, and I try to do that every night."

By doing nothing more than his job to the very best of his ability, Thompson eventually joined fellow Canadians like Bill Wennington, Rick Fox and his good friend Cory Joseph as only the sixth player from the country Steve Nash put on the basketball map for good, to ever win an NBA championship. Cleveland's adopted son would also remain a legend in the 216 for showing up and showing out in pursuit of a championship moment he knew his city so desperately deserved.

"To me I value him at a high level," Tyronn Lue said of Thompson in response to his top reserve being overlooked in the NBA Sixth Man of the Year voting—finishing a head-scratching 10th after averaging eight points and nine rebounds during the regular season for the Eastern Conference's best team. "I don't care what other teams think, what other people think about him. This team and myself, I value him at a high level and he's the pulse of our team as far as what we want to do offensively and defensively."

Where Thompson ever ranks as an individual is a mere footnote to who he has grown to become throughout his first five years in Cleveland. Unlike any Cavalier before him, he has made himself consistently available for a team he believes in above all else. And when his city needed help collecting that elusive title, Tristan Trevor James Thompson was there to go up and get it. ∎

Tristan Thompson was a force defensively and on the glass throughout the season and the playoffs, living up to the extension he signed before the 2015-2016 season.

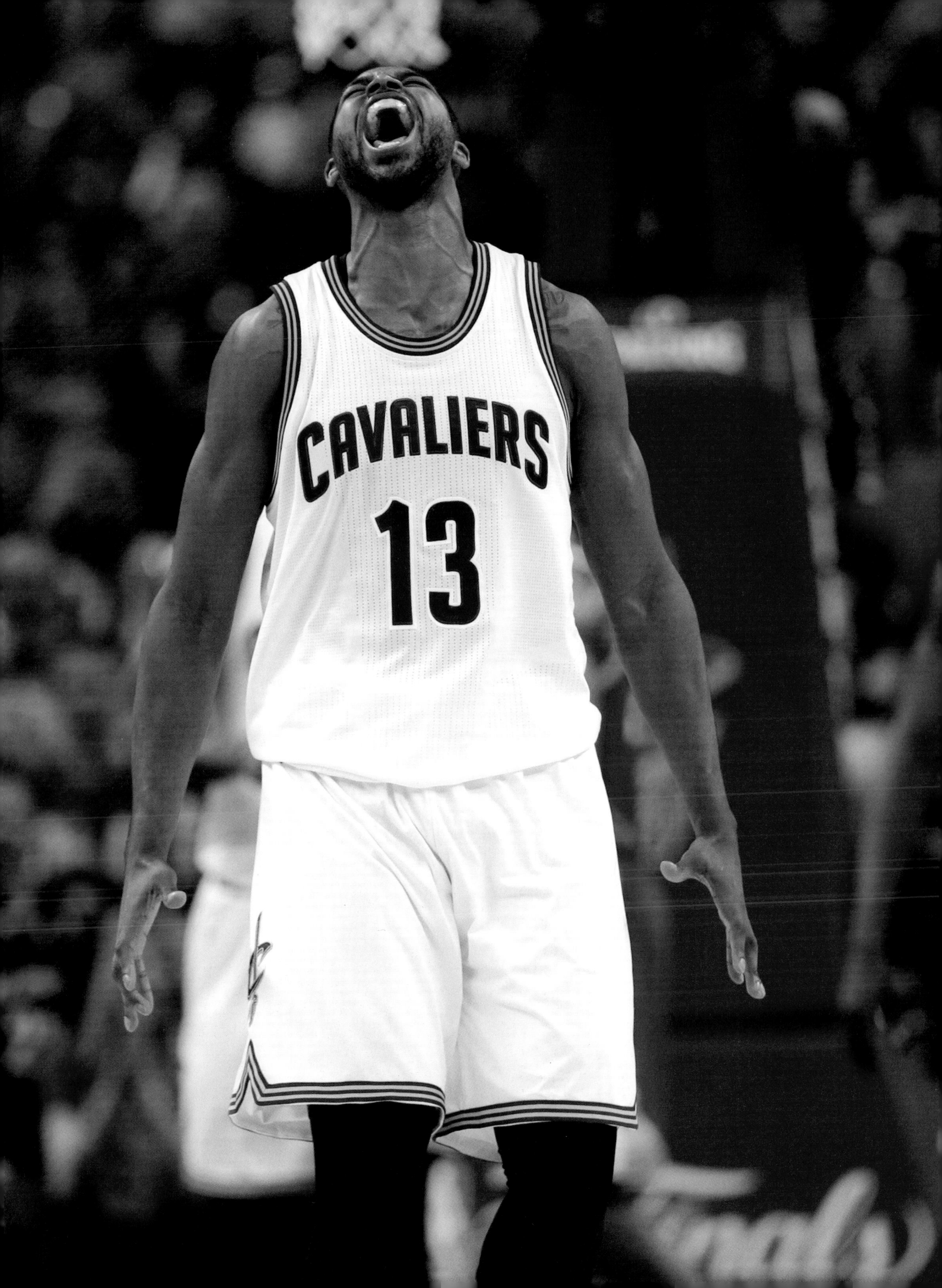
CAVALIERS
13

PLAYER PROFILE

24
SMALL FORWARD
RICHARD JEFFERSON

In a League Full of 'Veteran Leaders,' Jefferson Stands Out

When Seth Davis used the pages of *Sports Illustrated* in August of 1997 to introduce the basketball world to a young prospect named Richard Jefferson, Kyrie Irving was five years old. While the 6-7 forward was helping his Arizona Wildcats to the 2001 NCAA title four years later, Kevin Love was in junior high. And by the time LeBron James was breaking into the NBA as an 18-year-old rookie, the west Phoenix native had already teamed with Jason Kidd and the New Jersey Nets to earn a pair of Eastern Conference titles. Thirteen years later, Jefferson would lean on those lessons learned in a lifetime of basketball to help Irving, Love, James and the Cleveland Cavaliers grow into champions together.

"In my 15 years in the league, and all the basketball I've played in my life, I've thought a lot about team chemistry," Jefferson wrote in an article published by The Players' Tribune on the eve of Game 6 of the NBA Finals. "How do you come together at the right time? I've been on Finals teams and I've been on teams that had no chance to make the playoffs by midseason.

"To me, this season — and our team — comes down to narratives. All year long we heard about chemistry issues. LeBron and Kevin. Narrative. Kyrie's injury. Narrative. We got a new coach. Narrative. Oh, we're not getting along. Based on what? Who was telling our story? Not us. It's O.K. for others to speculate, but those narratives didn't show us as we really were."

Who the Cavaliers really were—and ultimately became—had as much to do with Jefferson's impact off the court as it did on it. His statistical output—while impressive at an age of 35 when most of his classmates are retiring from Sunday morning softball leagues—was pedestrian at best. The five points and two rebounds he averaged during nearly 18 minutes of work were a far cry from the 19 and six that he posted from 2002-09 while establishing himself as one of the best players of his era to never make an All-Star game. But Jefferson's ability to understand how a team comes together and his dedication to making that happen, would prove to be paramount in crafting the championship narrative Cleveland always hoped to read.

Whether chemistry issues existed or not early on in the season, it's fair to suggest that the Cavs provided at least some cause for speculation. The body language wasn't always good. The coach was fired in the middle

Veteran Richard Jefferson had a limited role in the regular season, averaging 18 minutes per game, but was a key factor in the NBA Finals. His insertion into the starting lineup allowed the Cavs to match the smaller lineups that the Warriors are known for.

of the season with his team in first place. The hero ball that plagued them at times certainly demonstrated a lack of connectivity. Some of the Twitter posts were odd. Added together, even on a team that won 56 games, they suggested at least the makings of a crack in the Cavaliers' foundation. But Jefferson would never let their championship spirit sink.

The Snapchat chronicles of 'Lil Kev' streaming live on RJeff24 were funny. They provided fans an exclusive look into the Cavaliers' locker room and demonstrated an engaging side of Jefferson that most NBA fans had never known during his 15 years in the league. But what Jefferson was also doing was working to help bring his team together at just the right time.

While faced with the stress of a championship-or-bust directive, RJ and Lil Kev kept things light because he knew that was important. Jefferson knew that the basketball journey and evolution of elite chemistry required a playful camaraderie. He knew his teammates couldn't take their brands or themselves so seriously that they forgot to laugh together. In the narrative that he was helping to write, he knew the Cavaliers must evolve from teammates to brothers.

The "veteran leadership" term is tossed around the NBA so liberally these days that it's a hard cliché to not simply dismiss. If a player has spent the better part of a decade on any team that accomplished some modicum of winning, the franchise who signs that player will reference this intangible benefit by glossing him with the veteran leadership tag at the introductory presser.

But when Cavaliers general manager David Griffin was searching for a piece to add locker room stability and production off the bench heading into the 2015-16 campaign, he signed the truest, role-playing, veteran leader to ever wear a Cavaliers uniform. When the Richard Jefferson narrative eventually concludes, Cleveland will always remember him for that. ∎

Known as a scorer earlier in his career, Jefferson earned his minutes on the Cavs with stingy and intelligent defense, timely scoring, and quick decision making with the ball.

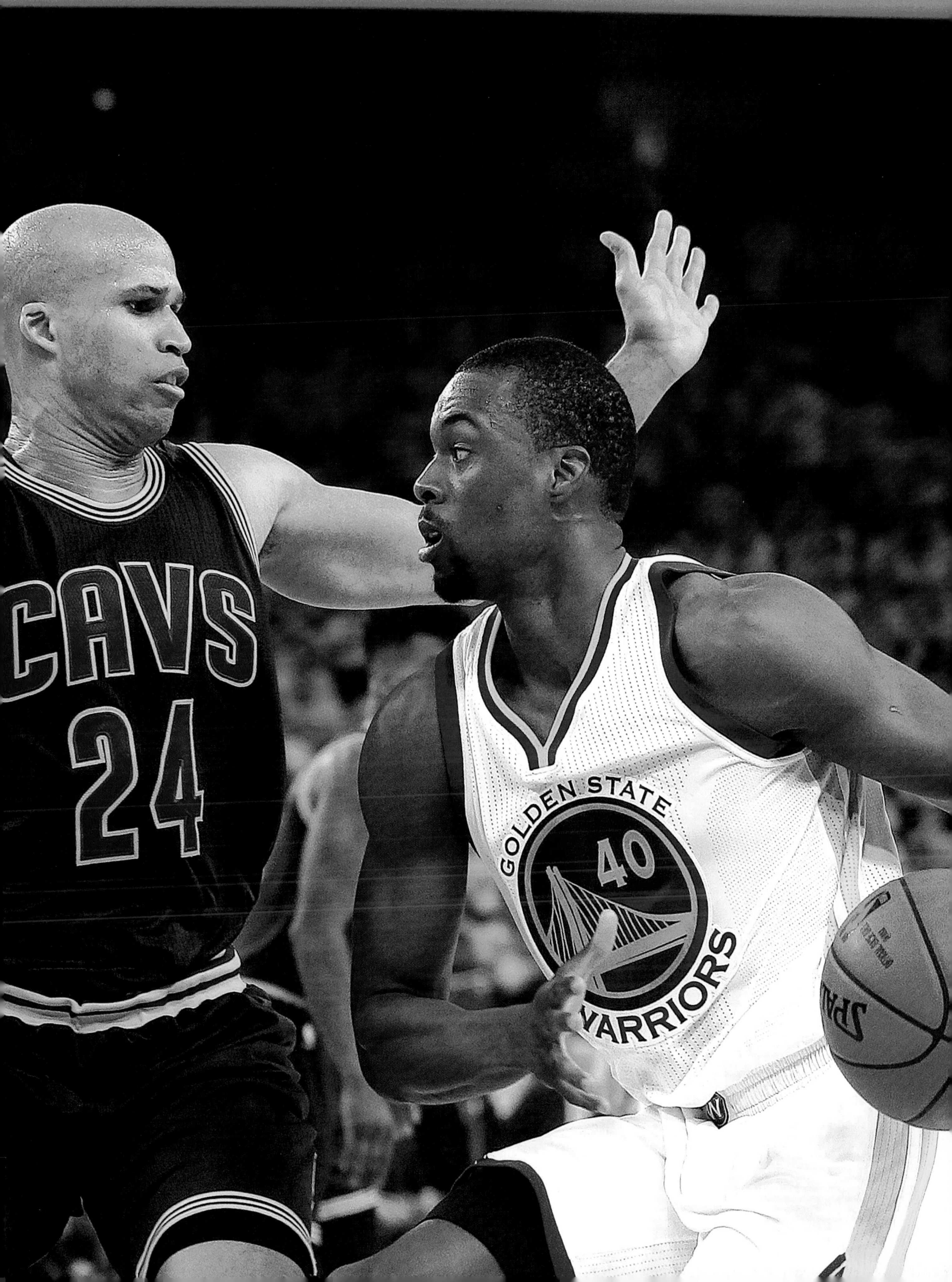
CAVS
24
GOLDEN STATE
40
WARRIORS

COACH

TYRONN LUE

Passed Over No More, Lue Guides Cavs to Greatness

Tyronn Lue first entered the NBA out of the University of Nebraska as the 23rd overall selection in the 1998 Draft. He'd play for eight teams over the next 10 seasons, helping Shaquille O'Neal and Kobe Bryant secure two NBA championships as a reserve guard for the Los Angeles Lakers. The scrappy floor general would retire with career averages of 8.5 points and 3.1 assists before the coaching chapter of his basketball journey began under the direction of Doc Rivers.

By the time Lue joined Rivers' staff—first in Boston and then with the Los Angeles Clippers—the pride of Mexico, Missouri had already secured the American dream. As an undersized guard in a league filled with giants, he earned millions of dollars along with the universal respect of his peers. Despite that success, however, his playing days would be most remembered in our Internet era for being famously stepped over by the great Allen Iverson. But even though he'd be passed over again in 2014 when the Cleveland Cavaliers came looking for their next head coach, Lue would eventually step into a new moment that immortalized his true place in basketball history.

"What I see is that we need to build a collective spirit, a strength of spirit, a collective will," Cavaliers general manager Griffin explained during a press conference that announced the firing of Cavs head coach David Blatt on January 22, 2016. "Elite teams always have that, and you see it everywhere. To be truly elite, we have to buy into a set of values and principles that we believe in. That becomes our identity."

Lue—the Cavaliers' top assistant at the time—would be tapped by Griffin to replace Blatt in search of that identity, and improve on an NBA Finals run that was followed by a 30-11 mark when he assumed the head coaching role. Without a training camp and minimal practice time, he would be tasked with accomplishing the only goal that Blatt never did in the middle of a championship-or-bust season.

"I am more than confident that he has the pulse of our team and that he can generate the buy-in required to start to refine the habits and culture that we've yet to build," Griffin added of Lue, and his head coaching career began.

Two months after Lue's transition from the highest-paid assistant in the NBA to head coach of the Eastern Conference's best team, the returns—on the surface—appeared minimal at best. Following a

Tyronn Lue was promoted at mid-season from his associate head coach position to replace fired head coach David Blatt. Lue went 27-14 during the regular season and helped the Cavs sprint through the playoffs to a 16-5 record and NBA title.

blowout loss to the Miami Heat where his team gave up 122 points, the Cavs had dropped to NBA rankings of 14th in defensive rating and 20th in defensive field-goal percentage from fifth and ninth, respectively, under Blatt. His rotations remained consistently inconsistent, and the quickened pace he promised to inspire was yet to materialize. But LeBron James would eventually close the regular season playing some of the best basketball of his Cavaliers career, and Cleveland began trending upward at just the right time.

The Cavaliers ripped through the Eastern Conference Playoffs with a high-octane offensive attack they were never able to ignite under Blatt. According to Richard Jefferson's SnapChat, and everything we could see from a high-fiving bench filled with more secret handshakes than Gatorade, the collective spirit of the Cavs had also begun to transform. But that spirit would face its greatest test as Game 3 of the NBA Finals approached.

After being thoroughly out-coached by Golden State's Steve Kerr and falling behind 2-0 in the series, Lue remained confident in both his team and strategy. He continued to employ a small-ball lineup featuring Jefferson in Kevin Love's starting spot, and willed his team to beat the Warriors at the very brand of basketball they made famous—and they'd respond like champions.

"First off, I want to say hello to Mexico, Missouri, where I'm from," Lue said as the postseason came to a close. "I want to just thank Dan, Jeff, Nate and David Griffin for putting together a great team like we have. Every night the Big Three, two of the three are going to play great every night. Then we need someone else to step up, and guys have been stepping up throughout the course of the season. Channing Frye, J.R. Smith, Dellavedova. Guys come in, they step up. It's not just the Big Three, it's a team effort."

A team effort that was reshaped in the image and spirit of an NBA champion, who would never be stepped over again. ■

Lue's title with the Cavs was the third of his career, winning two previously as a backup point guard for the Lakers in 2000 and 2001.

EASTERN CONFERENCE QUARTERFINALS

GAME 1: CAVALIERS 106, PISTONS 101
April 17, 2016 · Cleveland, Ohio

ELBOW WEDGE SHORT
Love Helps Cavs Avoid Game 1 Upset

Tyronn Lue had no intention of playing conservative in his first postseason appearance as the Cleveland Cavaliers' head coach. He proved as much with a radical adjustment in Game 1 of the Eastern Conference Quarterfinals that helped Cleveland overcome a late deficit and secure a 106-101 victory. Despite logging only 8.1 percent of his minutes at the center position during the regular season, that's precisely where Kevin Love was inserted with 11 minutes remaining and it changed the course of the game.

Down seven points to a Detroit Pistons team anchored by All-Star center Andre Drummond— who had defended the paint effectively throughout the contest—shifting Love to the 5 opened up much needed space around the rim. The Cavaliers ate off a steady diet of a play called "elbow wedge short" upon making the move, which forced Drummond away from the basket to defend Love at the high post. Love, LeBron James, Kyrie Irving and the rest of the Cavaliers capitalized from there, and closed the game with a dominating performance.

During those final 11 minutes, Love scored eight points, grabbed four rebounds and dished out an assist while fueling a 30-18 Cavs run that sealed the victory. Playing in his first postseason game since suffering a shoulder injury in the opening round of the 2015 playoffs, Love was aggressive and effective at both ends of the floor while finishing with a 28-point, 13-rebound night.

"Kevin at the 5 is tough for them to try to defend," Lue said after the game. "That play (elbow wedge short), I think we manufactured probably 10 points in a row just running that play alone. It was a big play for us and putting Kevin at the 5 was a big adjustment for us."

Led by Kentavious Caldwell-Pope (21 points), Marcus Morris (20 points) and Reggie Jackson (17 points), the upstart Pistons capitalized on the attention paid to their All-Star center inside offensively by knocking down 15 of 29 three-pointers. They built a halftime lead that was extended into the opening minutes of the fourth quarter before Lue made his critical adjustment. Irving, meanwhile—who suffered a season-ending injury during the 2015 NBA Finals—hit five threes while posting a game-high 31 points for Cleveland. To round out the Big Three's 81-point collective effort, James scored 22 to go along with 11 assists.

"Between Kyrie and myself, we've had many conversations about our playoff run being cut short," Love said postgame. "The way I look at it is an opportunity. I want to come out here, be really aggressive, have a next play type of mentality and just try to be one of the leaders out there and make an impact." ■

Kevin Love and Pistons center Aaron Baynes fight for position under the hoop. Love had a huge game, finishing with 28 points and a team-high 13 rebounds.

EASTERN CONFERENCE QUARTERFINALS

GAME 2: CAVALIERS 107, PISTONS 90
April 20, 2016 · Cleveland, Ohio

THREE FOR ALL

Cavs Hit 20 Three-Pointers To Tie NBA Record

LeBron James buried a deep three only a few feet away from the Detroit Pistons' bench during a 19-point second half run that turned a five-point Game 2 deficit into a 14-point lead for the Cleveland Cavaliers. As the ball drifted through the net, James turned in the direction of Stan Van Gundy while raising three fingers on each hand. The celebratory gesture would serve as an unofficial response to the public criticisms levied days earlier by the Pistons coach. It would also account for one of Cleveland's record-tying 20 three-pointers they'd knock down on the night.

"A couple calls have upset our guys," Van Gundy told ESPN during the Game 1 television broadcast. "They've got to understand, LeBron's LeBron. They're not going to call offensive fouls on him. He gets to do whatever he wants. They've got to understand that."

James didn't respond to Van Gundy when pressed by reporters, but his on-court statement said enough. He connected on 2 of 4 three-point field goals while posting a game-high 27 points. His effort helped the Cavaliers close the third quarter with a double-digit lead before cruising to a 107-90 win. After the game, King James applauded his team's efficiency on the offensive end.

"When the ball was moving like it was, and we got the shots we were getting, we can be satisfied with that," James said of Cleveland's performance in Game 2. "To be able to set an NBA record for threes made, it's great to be a part of history."

Eight Cavaliers connected on at least one three-pointer as J.R. Smith led the way with a game-high seven. Each of the field goals Smith converted for the game came from beyond the arc, as he finished with 21 points. In support of a 20-point effort from Andre Drummond—who paced the Pistons—Reggie Jackson chipped in 14 while Tobias Harris and Kentavious Caldwell-Pope each finished with 13 in a game that was never in doubt during the fourth quarter.

Matthew Dellavedova sparked the Cavaliers' second unit by coming off the bench to dish out a game-high nine assists to go along with eight points. Kyrie Irving knocked down four triples to finish with 22, Love posted a double-double with 16 and 10 and the Cavaliers closed the game by making 20 of the 38 three-point field goals they attempted during the record-tying performance.

"I was open so I shot the ball," the candidly honest Smith said after finishing 7-of-11 from three. "It's kind of simple for me. I have some great teammates who are willing to make the open pass, and I was just one of the guys in that situation to make them tonight." ■

J.R. Smith went off from three-point range, drilling seven and finishing with 21 points.

GAME 3: CAVALIERS 101, PISTONS 91
April 22, 2016 · Auburn Hills, Michigan

THE BIG THREE HITS THEIR STRIDE

Irving Ices Game From Corner

The outcome was still very much in doubt as Kyrie Irving stalked his target from the far corner with under a minute remaining in Game 3. But just as soon as he collected a pass from Matthew Dellavedova, Irving rose, fired, and released a dagger that would eliminate any question of a Cleveland Cavaliers victory. As the ball nestled through the rim, his three-point field goal gave Cleveland a 98-90 advantage that they'd eventually extend to a 101-91 win.

Following Irving's heroics, LeBron James met his young point guard at half-court with a celebratory chest bump. The scene made a sweep of the scrappy Detroit Pistons seem inevitable, as Cleveland's Big Three of James, Irving and Kevin Love continued to roll. Each of the Cavaliers' superstars would hit the 20-point scoring mark on the night, giving way to the sense that something truly special was beginning to take form.

"I think our preparation going into our second postseason, we know what to expect from one another," Irving said following the Game 3 win. "We're not necessarily concerned with the B.S. that's going on outside of the locker room. We know what to expect, we execute the game plan, and we are executing at a really high level on both ends of the floor."

Most of the chatter outside of the Cavs' locker room heading into Game 3 surrounded the Pistons rookie, Stanley Johnson. During the first two games of the series, Johnson shot the ball well going 4-of-5 from three and 7-of-11 from the floor overall. He logged 20 minutes per night, and did his best to compete defensively in a matchup with James. But by no stretch of the imagination did the rookie throw LeBron off his game, which is what the 19-year-old forward outlandishly suggested.

"I'm definitely in his head, that's for sure," Johnson told NBA.com of James following Game 2. "That's for sure."

In truth, he wasn't. James would go on to close out the series with averages of 22.8 points, nine rebounds and seven assists. But what was starting to enter the heads of NBA fans and pundits, was that the Cavaliers could be on the verge of playing their best stretch of basketball collectively at just the right time. Irving threw in a game-high 26 points in Game 3 while James and Kevin Love continued to make plays, each scoring 20 to go along with double-digit rebounds.

"For me, I had to continue to be aggressive," Love said following the win in Detroit. "These two guys over here (James and Irving) have been constantly on me about that. So, when they're coming to the double team I just face up to see what they are going to give me and make a play." ■

LeBron James and Kyrie Irving combined for 53 points in the Cavs' Game 4 win, with LeBron contributing 22 of those points, along with 11 rebounds and six assists.

EASTERN CONFERENCE QUARTERFINALS

GAME 4: CAVALIERS 100, PISTONS 98
April 24, 2016 · Auburn Hills, Michigan

ON TO THE NEXT ONE
Cavs Sweep Pistons, Advance to Second Round

LeBron James led the Cleveland Cavaliers in scoring during each round of the 2015 NBA Playoffs, averaging a team-high 30.1 points. Throughout the 2015-16 regular season, he also finished as Cleveland's scoring leader. But with the postseason emergence of a healthy Kyrie Irving and Kevin Love, it appeared support in the scoring column had arrived for James as the 2016 Eastern Conference Quarterfinals concluded.

While helping Cleveland eliminate the Detroit Pistons in a hard-fought, 100-98 Game 4 victory, Irving scored 31 points for the second time in the series. On the strength of that effort, he finished Round 1 of the postseason as the Cavs leading scorer with an average of 27.5. Irving used a 20-point second-half explosion to finalize the sweep, as LeBron collected 11 rebounds and matched his series average with 22 points. Love, J.R. Smith and Matthew Dellavedova each finished with double-figure points as well, while Love grabbed a game-high 13 rebounds.

"For our team, it doesn't matter who is the leading scorer or anything. We just want to get wins," James said following Game 4 in Detroit. "But the fact that (Kyrie) was in such a great groove, just throughout this whole series, we rode his coattails, we rode (Kevin Love), and I was able to focus on some other things, especially my rebounding, getting guys involved and defensively, just trying to lock in on my individual matchup."

In that final matchup, Marcus Morris (24 points), Tobias Harris (23 points) and Andre Drummond (17 points) combined to score 64 points in defeat. Reggie Jackson would have one final shot at extending the series as the game clock expired, but his desperation heave missed its mark. The Pistons demonstrated themselves well throughout, but they were simply out-gunned by the superior talent of the Cavaliers.

"The closeout game is the hardest one to win," Dellavedova said after an 11-point effort in Game 4. "It's been a tough, physical series the whole way through so definitely happy to get the win tonight."

The series victory positioned the Cavaliers to await the winner of the Boston Celtics and Atlanta Hawks in the Eastern Conference Semifinals. As the Cavs traveled home on April 24 to prepare for Round 2, the Celtics secured an overtime victory to tie their series at 2-2. It would be four more days of rest for King James and company before their next opponent was identified.

"Each series is different," Tyronn Lue said after Game 4. "You've got defensive schemes that are going to be different, so now everything's going to be different. But I think our guys did a good job overall with the series, it was a great series for us and it tested us." ∎

LeBron James and Kyrie Irving combined for 53 points in the Cavs' Game 4 win, with LeBron contributing 22 of those points, along with 11 rebounds, and six assists.

EASTERN CONFERENCE SEMIFINALS

GAME 1: CAVALIERS 104, HAWKS 93

May 2, 2016 · Cleveland, Ohio

THE BEAT GOES ON

Cavs Continue Dominance of Hawks with Game 1 Win

The Cleveland Cavaliers had every reason to be confident about their matchup with the Atlanta Hawks heading into Round 2. On the heels of sweeping the Hawks in the 2015 Eastern Conference Finals, the Cavs had won each of the three regular-season meetings between the two teams by an average of 10 points. They also moved past Atlanta in the playoffs a year earlier despite a season-ending injury to Kevin Love, and this time they'd be at full strength against the No. 4 seed in the East. Coming off a sweep of the Detroit Pistons, the momentum was most certainly on the side of the Cavaliers and the first quarter of Game 1 played out accordingly.

Anchored by All-Stars Paul Millsap and Al Horford up front, the Hawks featured the NBA's best defense statistically during the second half of the season. They also held a feisty Boston Celtics team they eliminated in six games under 39 percent shooting from the floor in Round 1. But unfortunately for Atlanta, none of that mattered to LeBron James and his army of assassins. The Cavs opened fire from long range in the first quarter, knocking down six three-pointers on their way to earning a 30-19 lead heading into the second period.

J.R. Smith launched the attack by connecting on a deep three less than one minute into the game. James, Kyrie Irving and Channing Frye would also triple during the opening session, and a frenzied crowd inside Quicken Loans Arena offered an electric response. While attempting to run the Hawks right out of the gym from there, Tyronn Lue introduced a new wrinkle to the rotation as the second quarter began that would go on

to pay major dividends later on in the series.

Despite playing sparingly in Round 1, Lue subbed Frye into a second-quarter group that included James, Matthew Dellavedova, Richard Jefferson and Iman Shumpert. It was the first time Cleveland unleashed their Midwest version of the Golden State Warriors' "Death Lineup" during a critical spot in the postseason, and the unit helped quicken the pace while holding onto a 10-point lead at the break. But a proud Hawks team coached by Mike Budenholzer would punch back in the third.

Sparked by reserve guard Dennis Schroder—who finished with a game-high 27 points—the Hawks pieced together a 24-7 run from the end of the third quarter through the beginning of the fourth. With eight minutes remaining in the game, Horford collected a lob pass from Schroder and slammed it home to bring Atlanta all the way back with an 80-79 lead. The game remained tied with four minutes to play, but then the Cavaliers answered with a championship-caliber run of their own that ended all hope for the ATL. Led by James, Smith and Love, Cleveland erased what quickly became a double-digit deficit to close out the game on a 17-2 run that secured a 104-93 victory.

"I think at the end of the day, we are going to learn from the mistakes that we made tonight," James said of letting their lead evaporate in the second half. "The best thing about our team is that we will make adjustments going into Game 2 and we'll learn from what we could have done much better. I think we played an okay game,

Tristan Thompson battles Hawks forward Paul Millsap for the rebound. Thompson dominated the glass, snagging 14 rebounds in the Cavs' Game 1 victory.

but I don't think we played to our standards."

At one of the most critical moments of the night, the streaky-shooting Smith stepped up for Cleveland by calmly knocking down one of his four three-pointers with 4:06 remaining. The clutch shot from the guy they call "Swish" gave the Cavaliers a 90-88 lead and they never looked back. Two minutes later, James converted a three-point play and flexed in celebration on his way to the free-throw line as the crowd roared. LeBron finished with a team-high 25 points to go along with nine rebounds and seven assists. Love added 17 points and 11 rebounds, Kyrie Irving scored 21 while dishing out eight assists, Smith finished with 12 and Tristan Thompson collected a game-high 14 boards.

"I thought they did a great job of mixing it up," Lue said of his team's 17-2 run to close the game. "Kevin (Love) stayed with it and made some big shots for us down the stretch. That's what our team is. Every night, there's going to be someone different stepping up and making a big shot. J.R. (Smith) made a big shot for us too when we were down one. That's just the confidence that we have in each other." ∎

EASTERN CONFERENCE SEMIFINALS

GAME 2: CAVALIERS 123, HAWKS 98
May 4, 2016 · Cleveland, Ohio

ON FIRE

Cavs' Historic Three-Point Shooting Knocks Hawks Out Early

The three-point shot had been an effective weapon for the Cleveland Cavaliers throughout the regular season. But it never had the same nuclear effect as it did for the 73-win Golden State Warriors. The Cavs finished seventh in the NBA behind the league-leading Warriors at 36.2 percent from three on the year, making an average of 10.7 triples per contest. During Game 2 of the Eastern Conference Semifinals, however, Cleveland would erupt into NBA Jam mode while hoisting fireballs from all over the court.

Less than two weeks after Golden State set an NBA playoff record with 21 three-pointers in the Western Conference Quarterfinals against the Houston Rockets, Cleveland eclipsed that total by knocking down 25. The mark—14 more than their season average—was not only a new playoff high, but also the most three-pointers made by any team in NBA history including the regular season. The let-it-fly guard J.R. Smith led the onslaught for Cleveland while playing in the type of free-flowing game he most certainly dreamed of growing up on the playgrounds of New Jersey. His spectacular shooting display helped build a stunning 36-point lead at halftime before finishing off a 123-98 drubbing.

Kyrie Irving and LeBron James each made four three-pointers themselves while Kevin Love connected on three. For the game, 10 Cavaliers made at least one triple to contribute to the record-setting performance. Cleveland led by 15 after the first quarter and went on to make 18 three-pointers as a team before halftime. The only thing the Hawks could do in response was watch.

"We had great ball movement and player movement which we have been stressing all year," James said after the historic performance. "The ball finds the energy and guys were flying around today offensively. We have some guys that can make shots from the perimeter."

The Cavs finished 25-of-45 as a team from beyond the arc, shooting a stifling 55 percent from long-range. They also came one attempt shy of the most three-pointers ever attempted in a playoff game. Smith did most of his damage in the first half, turning in a dizzying string of turn-around jumpers and off-balance threes while making six of his seven in the first two quarters. The dominant performance and gaping point-differential even prompted the Hawks official Twitter account to use the "Crying Jordan" meme in lieu of Atlanta's point total for their halftime score update.

"When they put those shots down, I don't know if anyone can beat them, to be honest," Atlanta's three-point specialist Kyle Korver said following the game. "We were just hoping that they'd start missing at some point."

The Cavaliers never did start missing, and rode an historic shooting performance to their easiest victory of the postseason. James finished with a game-high 27 points while passing Tim Duncan for fifth on the career playoff scoring list. Smith finished with 23 points as his backcourt mate Irving threw in 19. Love posted another double-double with 11 points and 13 rebounds, as the Cavaliers starters sat for the majority of the second half. Meanwhile, Paul Millsap paced the shell-shocked Hawks with 16 points to go along with 11 rebounds.

"I think today's performance is a credit to just how hard we work," Smith said after the game. "We work

LeBron James swings the ball to a teammate during the Cavs' 123-98 rout of the Hawks. LeBron had 27 points in the game, hitting four three-pointers along the way.

on our shots every day and we are all very competitive with each other when it comes to shooting. I'm glad it happened, but we just can't settle and we have to keep moving on."

The Cavaliers attempted eight three-pointers during the fourth quarter with their rotation players resting before Dahntay Jones connected on the record-breaking 24th triple with 2:22 remaining. In response to the lopsided defeat—and perceived notion that the Cavs were attempting to embarrass Atlanta by shooting for the record—TNT analyst Charles Barkley suggested the Hawks should retaliate by "taking someone out" as retribution.

"You've got to take somebody out," Barkley said during the TNT postgame broadcast following Game 2. "When a team is just embarrassing you, shooting threes when the game is way over, just trying to set a record. You have to knock the heck out of them. Not for this game; to set the tone for the next game." ■

EASTERN CONFERENCE SEMIFINALS

GAME 3: CAVALIERS 121, HAWKS 108
May 6, 2016 • Atlanta, Georgia

SWEEP IN SIGHT

Frye's Career Night Puts the Cavs on the Brink of Another Sweep

Channing Frye etched his name in Cleveland Cavaliers folklore with an Eastern Conference Semifinals performance in Game 3 that maybe only general manager David Griffin saw coming. Cleveland acquired the 32-year-old Frye from the Orlando Magic at the trade deadline on February 18. The three-team deal raised more eyebrows around Cleveland at the time for the departure of Anderson Varejao—who was included along with Jared Cunningham and a conditional first-round draft pick as compensation for Frye—than it did for the addition of the 6-11 sharp-shooter. But as the final buzzer sounded on May 6 in Atlanta, Frye had closed the book on a deadline decision that would be applauded for decades.

During 29 regular season games, Frye averaged 7.5 points off the bench for the Cavaliers. In the first round against the Detroit Pistons, however, he fell completely out of coach Tyronn Lue's rotation. Frye averaged less than 10 minutes per night against Detroit, scoring a grand total of three points in four games. But against the Atlanta Hawks, his production began to slowly climb. He scored eight points in nine minutes during Game 1 and followed that up with 12 points on 5-of-7 shooting in Game 2 before exploding for an epic performance.

After scoring nine points in eight minutes during a scorching hot stretch in the first half, Lue called Channing's number again in the third quarter following Kevin Love's fourth foul. The Cavaliers trailed by 11 points with 9:09 remaining in the third as Frye knocked down a three-pointer, banked home a 15-footer and finished off a two-handed flush at the rim to help cut

the deficit to six heading into the fourth. He was only getting started from there.

Frye continued the lights-out shooting display by scoring 11 more points in the fourth quarter, going 3-of-3 from deep and 4-of-4 from the floor overall in the period—and the Cavaliers needed every one of those baskets. He finished with a career playoff high of 27 points on 10-of-13 shooting from the field, drilling 7-of-9 shots from distance. Frye's effort—along with a strong fourth quarter from Kyrie Irving—helped Cleveland to a 32-17 romp in the final period that ended in a 121-108 victory. More importantly, however, Frye's breakout game also demonstrated to the Cavaliers and NBA at large that Lue had yet another weapon at his disposal that could continue to cause matchup problems throughout the postseason.

"That's what we brought him here for," LeBron James said postgame in response to Frye's career night. "Sometimes he feels himself that even when he's open he wants to keep the ball moving, but we brought him here to shoot—shoot, shoot and shoot. Tonight he did exactly that and he gave us a huge boost. Obviously, he earned the game ball for our team."

While helping Atlanta build a third quarter lead, Jeff Teague scored 19 points and dished out 14 assists. Al Horford paced the Hawks with 24 and Paul Millsap added 17, but the opposing bigs had no answer for the outside shooting of Frye. Meanwhile, Irving saved his best stretch of basketball on the night for the final period. With James encouraging Irving to "hit the reset button" on the tough start as the fourth quarter began,

Kevin Love greets fans as he heads to the locker room after another dominant Cavs win over the Hawks, 121-108. Love chipped in 21 points and a team-high 15 rebounds.

the Cavaliers' point guard totaled 12 points to close the game while finishing with 24.

To open the final period, Irving and Frye combined on 14-straight points to help propel Cleveland to the victory. They took a 104-103 lead with 6:23 remaining after a LeBron three, and never relinquished the lead again. In the shadow of Frye's heroics, and Irving's late-game surge, James registered a workmanlike near triple-double with 24 points, 13 rebounds and eight assists while converting 50 percent of his field goals. Kevin Love battled through foul trouble to add 21 points and

15 boards in less than 30 minutes of work.

"We knew (the Hawks) were going to play well," Love said. "We had to withstand their run. They got up double-digits on us, and we had to just keep fighting. (The win) wouldn't have been possible without everybody, but Kyrie and Channing were amazing. We were able to keep it together, got the stops when we needed to, and really hit some big ones down the stretch." ∎

EASTERN CONFERENCE SEMIFINALS

GAME 4: CAVALIERS 100, HAWKS 99
May 8, 2016 · Atlanta, Georgia

PERFECT THROUGH EIGHT

Love and the Cavs Sweep Their Second Series in a Row

The Cleveland Cavaliers were on the verge of sweeping a playoff series from the Atlanta Hawks for the third straight time heading into Game 4. Prior to the 4-0 win during the 2015 Eastern Conference Finals, the Cavaliers had also swept their previous matchup in 2009. But as opposed to the way that LeBron James was forced to carry the scoring burden entirely on his shoulders for Cleveland seven years ago, this time around he had plenty of help. With the postseason emergence of a healthy Kyrie Irving and Kevin Love, Cleveland looked every bit the title contender its fan base had dreamed of when James returned in 2014.

Love worked inside and out while throwing in 27 points and grabbing 13 rebounds on the Cavaliers way to earning a hard-fought, 100-99, victory in Atlanta to close out the 2016 Eastern Conference Semifinals. Kyrie Irving dished out eight assists while making good on 8 of 16 field goal attempts to finish with 21. Love and Irving would combine to average just over 40 points, 14 rebounds and nine assists for the series. James, meanwhile, would take care of the rest by posting nine rebounds, eight assists and 24 points per night during the four games against the Hawks—10 points less than he was forced to average during their series in 2009. But the Hawks would give Cleveland everything they could handle in Game 4, refusing to go quietly into the offseason.

Dennis Schroder—who finished with a team-high 21 points for Atlanta—connected on a driving layup with 1:31 remaining to give his team a 97-96 lead over the visiting Cavaliers. But just as the Hawks fans rose to their feet in anticipation of a possible victory, James would answer with three critical plays that proved otherwise. The first came as LeBron responded to the go-ahead basket by converting a layup of his own off a feed from Matthew Dellavedova. He'd then knock down a fade away jumper to extend Cleveland's lead to 100-97, before blocking the Hawks final field goal attempt to take the lead with 2.8 seconds left.

"Well, we know Atlanta is a tough team and the closeout game is the hardest game," Cavs coach Tyronn Lue said after the game. "They gave us everything they had. We just stuck with it and stuck with the game plan. If we had to adjust we made adjustments. I think it felt good to get a win like that, especially on the road. Coming together, being down one with a 1:13 left in the game, we were able to win the game, and that's a big win for us."

The Hawks led by nine after the first quarter and clung to a two-point lead at the break. Cleveland retook a one-point advantage heading into the fourth before securing the victory. Iman Shumpert used two three-pointers to finish with 10 points on the night, while Tristan Thompson collected 10 more rebounds. In support of a team-high effort from Schroder, Paul Millsap finished with 19 points and Al Horford totaled 15.

"I know the guys have been waiting for this opportunity, being a part of the postseason again after what happened last year with their injuries," James said of Love and Irving after the game. "We're in a great rhythm right now as far as us three. We know exactly where we

LeBron James elevates to the rim while Atlanta forwards Paul Millsap (4), Kent Bazemore (24), and Thabo Sefolosha (25) look on. LeBron just missed out on a triple-double, with 21 points, 10 rebounds, and nine assists, as the Cavs swept the Hawks and moved on to the Eastern Conference Finals.

want to be on the floor. We know exactly where we are on the floor. It's benefited all of us individually and obviously it's trickled down to the team."

As the Cavaliers secured their second-straight berth in the Eastern Conference Finals, the Miami Heat and Toronto Raptors were battling it out to be their next opponent. One day after Cleveland eliminated Atlanta, Dwyane Wade would lead the Heat to a 94-87 victory to even the series at 2-2. It would not be until May 15— one full week after the Cavaliers second round series

concluded—until that series was decided.

"I think we did a good job between the last series sweep of us staying locked in," Love said in anticipation of preparing for the next round. "We did a great job of staying sharp on the court. We even had off-the-court, our team dinners, staying together as a team in every single way. So I feel like we're going to do a good job of that this week, being able to stay locked in and, for whatever is next, we're going to be ready." ∎

EASTERN CONFERENCE FINALS

GAME 1: CAVALIERS 115, RAPTORS 84
May 17, 2016 · Cleveland, Ohio

NEW ROUND, SAME RESULT
Cavs Romp Over Raptors in Game 1

LeBron James sized up DeMarre Carroll from the left corner with 7:29 remaining in the second quarter of Game 1 of the Eastern Conference Finals. After shifting the basketball from right to left, James exploded past his defender along the baseline. He dribbled twice before taking flight, leaping from behind the basket to deliver a thunderous tomahawk finish with an outstretched right hand. As the yellow, taxi-styled version of his signature Nikes touched down, the Cleveland Cavaliers bench erupted alongside 20,562 fans inside Quicken Loans Arena.

The aerial assault punctuated a 20-2 Cavs run that extended their first half lead to 47-30 over the visiting Toronto Raptors. James would total 24 points in 28 minutes, making nine consecutive field goals to open the game, on a night where he missed only twice. In response to the Raptors' defensive game plan of running Cleveland off the three-point line, James and company countered with 56 points in the paint. They built a 22-point halftime lead that grew to as many as 35 before the largest postseason win in Cavaliers franchise history was finalized, 115-84.

"I think for us, our game plan is never dictated," James said postgame of Cleveland's decision to attack the basket more frequently than they did while setting records from three-point range in the previous rounds. "We want to push the tempo. We want to move the ball from side to side, and we want to attack. With myself and Ky, we love to live in the paint. We love to attack, and then when the defense collapses, we're going to spread out to our shooters."

The defense never did collapse and the Cavaliers took full advantage by connecting on shot after shot from point-blank distance. Kyrie Irving joined James in relentless pursuit of the rim by slashing his way to 27 points on 11-of-17 shooting. He elevated his performance on the defensive end as well, helping to hold Toronto's All-Star backcourt of DeMar DeRozan and Kyle Lowry to only 26 points on 13-of-31 field goals combined for the game.

"We were just taking what the defense gave us," Irving said following Game 1. "It was as simple as that. We were getting to our sweet spots as much as possible and the play calls by Coach Lue were great. Coming out of timeouts we knew what we wanted to run and we played at an unbelievable place. At one point I looked up and Bron was 7-for-7, just an unbelievable pace and unbelievable rhythm. We wanted to just stick to that game plan."

The Cavs had nine days of rest heading into the

LeBron James tries to drive past Toronto forward DeMarre Carroll during the Cavs' Game 1 blowout of the Raptors. LeBron had a terrific shooting day, going 11-of-13 from the floor, for 24 points.

Eastern Conference Finals following their elimination of the Atlanta Hawks in Round 2. Instead of coming out lethargic, searching to regain their rhythm, Cleveland returned at a collective speed that Toronto could simply not match. After going seven games to eliminate the Indiana Pacers in Round 1, the Raptors needed seven more to move past Dwyane Wade and the Miami Heat while advancing to their first Eastern Conference Finals in franchise history. The physical and mental grind required along the way took its toll on the No. 2 seed in the East, and Cleveland capitalized by cruising to its ninth straight playoff victory with little resistance.

In support of a team-high 18 points from DeRozan, and an eight-point night from Lowry, Bismack Biyombo added 12 along with collecting four rebounds while starting in place of injured center Jonas Valanciunas. No other Raptor reached double figures besides James Johnson who came off the bench to score 10. Meanwhile, Kevin Love chipped in 14 for Cleveland as the Cavaliers starters watched much of the second half action from the bench. Richard Jefferson led the reserve unit with a game-high 11 boards, while he and Matthew Dellavedova each scored nine. Channing Frye hit two more threes and Iman Shumpert drilled one as they tossed in eight points apiece.

"I thought they were the fresher team, the quicker team tonight, to their credit," Raptors head coach Dwane Casey admitted following the 31-point loss in Cleveland to open the series. "It's one game. The series is not over by any means. We have another game in another night. The score is embarrassing, but it's just one game." ■

Kevin Love backs down Raptors forward Patrick Patterson. Love had 14 points in the Cavs' ninth straight playoff win.

GAME 2: CAVALIERS 108, RAPTORS 89

May 19, 2016 • Cleveland, Ohio

THE ROLL CONTINUES

LeBron and the Cavs Dominate the Raptors Again

The Cleveland Cavaliers' championship stock continued to rise in Game 2 of the Eastern Conference Finals. LeBron James added a 15th career postseason triple-double to his blue chip portfolio while surging past Shaquille O'Neal for fourth all-time on the playoff scoring list. He helped Tyronn Lue eclipse legendary bench boss Pat Riley for the most consecutive playoff wins to open a coaching career, as Cleveland continued its rally with a 19-point beat-down of the Toronto Raptors that was never in doubt during the second half.

To complement a 23-point, 11-rebound and 11 assists night from James, Kyrie Irving added a game-high 26 points while Kevin Love accounted for 19. It was business as usual for the Cleveland conglomerate that led by 14 at halftime before disposing the Raptors 108-89 at the closing bell. The frustrations boiled over for the No. 2 seed in the East with 2:35 remaining in the second quarter as Kyle Lowry retreated to the locker room in search of answers. He'd return to finish the game 4-of-14 from the floor overall and 1-of-8 from three as his team dropped their second-straight to the Cavs by a combined total of 50 points.

"Just to kind of decompress, get back there, kind of relax my body and relax my mind," Lowry replied to questions about why he left for the locker room, during his postgame media availability. "And knowing that we had a chance to kind of make some things [happen], I wanted to get myself going and get my teammates going and get the team going. It was nothing more than just kind of to decompress, breathe and get back out."

The Cavaliers never allowed the Raptors to catch their breath in the second half as the onslaught continued. Cleveland converted 64 percent of its field goals on the interior to finish with at least 50 points in the paint for the second straight night. They shot 50 percent from the field overall for the game, while limiting the Raptors to just 27 percent on 33 attempts from three-point range. DeMar DeRozan posted a team-high 22 points while Terrence Ross, Cory Joseph and James Johnson each added 11. Both teams would empty the bench with four minutes remaining as a third-straight postseason sweep for the Cavaliers appeared imminent.

"I just want to come out and play well for my teammates," Irving said of his effort on both ends of the floor in Game 2. "And it starts with our preparation on off days and shootaround. I just think we do a great job of having each other's backs, and it just makes our job a lot easier out there. We know what to expect. But this

LeBron draws the foul in the lane from Toronto guard Kyle Lowry. The Cavs won big over the Raptors — 108-89 — for the second straight game, and LeBron posted his 15th playoff triple-double.

is high-intensity basketball that we've all been waiting for, and to all be healthy at the same time and doing whatever it takes to win. This is what we want to be part of and we've been waiting for."

During a February 26 matchup with Irving and the Cavs, Lowry led Toronto to a two-point victory while posting a season-high 43 points on 75 percent shooting. Irving's ability to compete defensively against the All-Star point guard was very much a question heading into the conference finals. But he responded admirably to open the series by helping to limit Lowry to 29 percent shooting from the floor overall and only 1-of-15 from three in the first two contests. Gary Payton he most certainly was not, but Irving was doing enough to make life difficult for the Raptors' floor general. As the Cavaliers continued to check every box on their 10-0 romp through the playoffs, the year-end dividend seemed as promising as ever.

"It's been great," Lue said in response to Cleveland's dominating run to begin the postseason. "You know, I just think—always just think back, coming from a small town in Mexico, Missouri, that I would ever be in a position that I'm in now today, and just a tribute to the organization, Dan Gilbert and the way they constructed this team, David Griffin, those guys have done a great job. We've just got a great team, and they're playing great basketball right now. We've just got to keep it going." ■

Kyrie Irving goes up for the layup with Raptors center Bismack Biyombo challenging. Irving was the leading scorer in the game with 26 points.

EASTERN CONFERENCE FINALS

GAME 3: RAPTORS 99, CAVALIERS 84
May 21, 2016 · Toronto, Ontario

PERFECTION THWARTED
DeRozan Erupts for 32, Gives Cavs First Loss of Playoffs

Maybe complacency set in for the first time during the Cleveland Cavaliers' 2016 playoff run. Maybe the crowd gathered at the Air Canada Centre both inside and out offered more of a home court advantage than anyone anticipated. Or, maybe the 56-win Toronto Raptors—who finished only two games behind the Cavs in the Eastern Conference standings—were simply much better than their two previous performances would indicate. Whatever the reason, Cleveland's edge never made it through Customs in Game 3. Toronto jumped on the Cavaliers early, building a 13-point advantage at halftime before climbing back into the series with a stunning victory, 99-84.

DeMar DeRozan showed out for the Raptors to lead all scorers with 32 points while doing all of his damage inside the three-point line. The 6-7 shooting guard used a combination of 18-foot jump shots, mid-range buckets, and hard drives through the Cavaliers defense to finish 12-of-24. On a night when "We The North" chants rang out all through Canada, Kyle Lowry bounced back to score 20 at home. The starting guards for Toronto combined to outduel Kyrie Irving and J.R. Smith 52-35 as a result, but the name that trended on Twitter was Bismack Biyombo.

The Cavaliers starting frontcourt of Tristan Thompson and Kevin Love had absolutely no answer for Biyombo. Starting in place of the injured Jonas Valanciunas for the third straight game in the series, the 23-year-old role player drafted eighth overall in 2011 ripped down a Toronto postseason record of 26 rebounds to go along with seven points. Thompson and Love combined to collect only 12 boards, totaling just three points between them. Biyombo would also wag his finger like the great Dikembe Mutombo after blocking four shots, helping to hold Cleveland to just 20 points in the paint after averaging 53 in Games 1 and 2.

"I think early on, at the start of the game, we weren't as physical as we should have been," LeBron James said after a 24-point, eight-rebound and five-assist performance in Game 3. "Especially coming into a building that we knew we had to be a little bit more physical. Understanding they were going to play with a lot of speed, a lot of force, so we didn't start the game as physical as we should have at the point of attack."

Thompson was held scoreless despite grabbing eight rebounds, and Love turned in the worst performance of his 15-game postseason career. He shot 1-of-9 from the floor, finishing with three points and four rebounds while not attempting a free throw.

Bismack Biyombo prepares to block LeBron James' shot in Toronto's 99-84 Game 3 win. LeBron scored 24 points but Biyombo was the story of the game, corralling 26 big rebounds.

Tyronn Lue benched Love in the fourth quarter in favor of Channing Frye, but he was hardly the only Cavaliers superstar to struggle. Irving registered a game-worst plus/minus of minus-14, while making only 3-of-19 field goal attempts. But it would be Love who received the majority of criticism from fans and media alike for his ineffective night following the loss.

"I think just being aggressive," Love said in response to how he was being played defensively in Game 3. "But I need to match that and be just as aggressive and tonight I wasn't, I felt like I was a little bit passive. I have to come out Monday night and just have that type of mentality and do better on that end. I feel like from a mentality standpoint it's an easy fix."

Love had scored double-figure points for 10 straight postseason games while posting eight double-doubles during that stretch prior to Game 3 in Toronto. But the change of mentality he hoped for would prove more difficult to find than he expected heading into Game 4. The Cavaliers did receive a solid effort from Smith, however, who knocked down six triples while scoring 22. Frye added 11 on 4-of-5 shots, but that was it for Cleveland. Cory Joseph, Patrick Patterson and DeMarre Carroll each reached double-figures for Toronto in support of the monster nights from DeRozan and Biyombo.

"They came out and it wasn't the same team that was in Cleveland," Thompson said after playing his first postseason game in his hometown of Toronto, Canada. "They came out and played hard. We knew that, and we expected that especially coming home, with the crowd so energetic. We just didn't match their energy." ∎

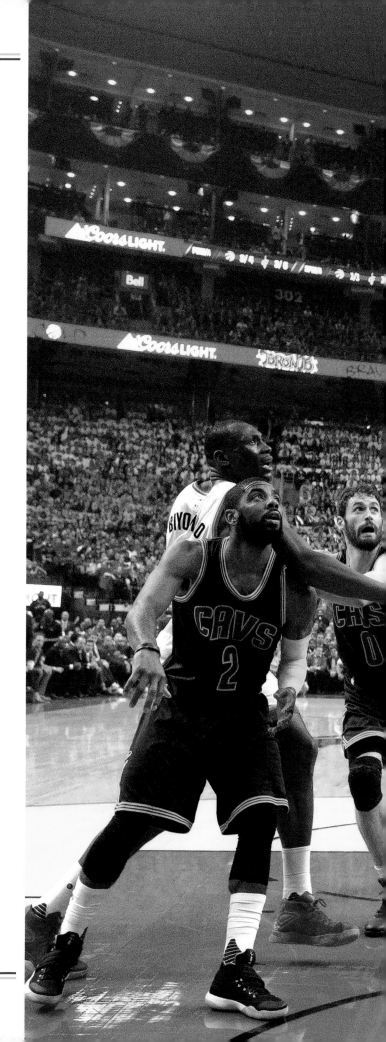

Tristan Thompson rejects the shot of Raptors guard Kyle Lowry. It was one of two blocks for Thompson, while Lowry dropped 20 points in the Raps victory.

EASTERN CONFERENCE FINALS

GAME 4: RAPTORS 105, CAVALIERS 99
May 23, 2016 • Toronto, Ontario

ALL TIED UP
Despite Furious Comeback by Cavs, Series Even at 2-2

The Cleveland Cavaliers opened Game 4 to the tune of a sad trombone by missing eight of their first 10 shots from the field. They'd also miss 18 times from three-point range before halftime, while allowing Kyle Lowry and DeMar DeRozan to combine for their highest scoring game ever as a duo. Despite being consistently torched off the bounce, however—and falling behind the Toronto Raptors by 16 at the break—Cleveland would nevertheless mount a furious charge to come all the way back in the fourth quarter.

The Cavaliers outscored the Raptors by 10 in the second half, erasing a deficit that reached as many as 18 before taking their first lead in the contest. But Toronto responded by making enough plays down the stretch to secure a 105-99 win to even the Eastern Conference Finals at 2-2. The Cavs' Big 3 were outscored 67-65 by Lowry (35) and DeRozan (32), as Kevin Love struggled on the road for the second straight night. LeBron James led Cleveland with 29 points while Kyrie Irving scored 26 but the early hole proved too deep to ultimately overcome.

"It wasn't enough because we got off to a horrible first half once again in this building, and you're playing catch-up the whole game," James said postgame of Cleveland's second-half comeback bid falling short. "So every defensive possession feels even more intensified when you've given up so many points in the first half. I think they've averaged 58 or something like that in the first half here, and in the high 30s the second half. We're not starting off games the right way."

For as bad as the Cavaliers started, they closed Game 4 by making 11 consecutive field goals to open a highly entertaining fourth quarter. Cleveland trailed 78-69 as the final period began before Channing Frye connected on back-to-back triples, fueling an 8-0 run to bring Cleveland within one. Tyronn Lue would ride the small-ball lineup of Richard Jefferson, Matthew Dellavedova, Iman Shumpert, Frye and James for most of the period, while the Cavs took their first lead of the night with 8:20 remaining. But the Raptors would inevitably capitalize on the smaller Cavs unit by grabbing a series of pivotal rebounds in the final minutes. As Bismack Biyombo finished off a 14-board effort, the Cavaliers simply ran out of gas. Lowry scored the final points in the game with a driving layup that gave Toronto the six-point victory as the series shifted back to Cleveland.

"I think we just started being a lot more aggressive, we started picking up the pace of the game," Frye said

Toronto guard DeMar DeRozan goes up for the layup in traffic. DeRozan and his backcourt mate Kyle Lowry combined for 67 points, as the Raptors evened the series at 2-2.

of the Cavs' fourth quarter comeback attempt where he scored nine of his 12 points on the night. "The ball started moving, we started getting really good shots, executing, we had a sense of urgency. Give them credit, they took care of home court and so we get to go back home."

The sense of urgency came too late for a Cleveland team that saw two of its starters—Love and J.R. Smith—combine to shoot just 7-of-26 for the game. Love's 4-of-14 performance was ended late in the third after he stepped awkwardly on a referee's foot and twisted his ankle. Whether he was healthy enough to return or not was unclear, and Lue offered little in terms of exactly why his superstar was benched for the second straight fourth quarter after the game.

"I'm not sure of his health, but there is no concern," Lue replied when asked for an update on Love's health as well as if there was any concern regarding his play over the last two games. "I thought Channing came in and gave us a great lift when we were down. And like I said, like last game, to try to put Kevin back in with four minutes to go in the fourth quarter in a hostile environment is not fair to him."

Fair or not, Love's critics would only get louder over the next two days as the Cavaliers prepared for Game 5. The way Love responded would be pivotal in determining just how likely a celebratory parade down Euclid Avenue might actually be at the end of the season. ■

Kyrie Irving attacks the basket while DeMare Carroll (5) and DeMar DeRozan (10) defend. Kyrie had 26 points but the Cavs dropped Game 4, 105-99.

EASTERN CONFERENCE FINALS

GAME 5: CAVALIERS 116, RAPTORS 78
May 25, 2016 • Cleveland, Ohio

ORDER RESTORED
Cavs Destroy Raps to Regain Control of the Series

Kevin Love shook off a disappointing trip to Toronto immediately upon entering Game 5 of the Eastern Conference Finals. He'd connect on his first four shots while opening with 12 points in the first quarter. Love would go on to finish 8-of-10 from the field overall, posting a game-high 25 points after managing only 13 in the two previous losses. He'd also drop a dime that would make Baby Dame proud, finding a streaking LeBron James on a two-handed, overhead missile from 50 feet away. Love's effort helped the Cleveland Cavaliers build the largest halftime lead in conference finals history before wrapping up a 116-78 decision over the Toronto Raptors.

Kyrie Irving helped fuel the 37-19 first quarter margin by adding 11 points in the opening period before completing a 23-point effort. LeBron James would also score 23, checking out of the game for good with the Cavs up 37 late in the third. The Big 3 totaled 71 points on a night where they sat the entire fourth quarter for all the right reasons. The Cavs lead would balloon to as many as 43 as they dominated the rebounding battle, 48-27, and led the Raptors by 31 at halftime.

"I think it was everybody locking in at home," Love said of the difference in this game compared to the previous two. "We let the games get away from us in Toronto, but they played well there. We are going to have a tough fight on our hands going back to their place. We have to do our best to try and close it out like we did tonight."

James, Irving and Love were most definitely locked in as they combined to outscore the Raptors 43-34 at intermission. Cleveland would lead by as many as 34 in the first half before finalizing the 38-point thrashing. The Cavaliers decision to blitz Kyle Lowry and DeMar DeRozan on pick-and-rolls, while going over the screen throughout the night, paid off as the two Raptors combined for just 7-of-20 field goals in the loss. Cleveland would also limit Toronto to just 3-of-17 shooting from three-point range, using their defense to get out in transition and help generate 21 fast break points.

"We understood that coming back from Game 3 and Game 4 we just didn't play our defense the right way," James told the media afterwards. "We didn't play how we should have played, and they took advantage of every moment. We had to get back to our staple. We had to get back to what we wanted to do defensively in order for us to play a complete game. That was the most satisfying thing, the way we defended, holding these guys to 39 percent shooting."

LeBron dunks emphatically while DeMare Carroll helplessly looks on. The Cavs re-established control of the series in resounding fashion with a 116-78 shellacking of the Raptors.

The Cavaliers' smothering defense helped hold every other Raptor besides DeRozan (14 points) and Lowry (13 points) under double-digits. If it's possible to have a bright spot while suffering a 30-point loss during the biggest game in franchise history, Jonas Valanciunas was it for the visiting Raptors. The talented 7-footer from Lithuania returned from injury to score nine points on 4-of-4 shooting in 18 minutes. But the rest was most certainly miserable for Dwane Casey and the thousands of Toronto fans standing outside the Air Canada Centre watching the embarrassing loss from a parking lot.

Richard Jefferson slapped the glass on a first-half dunk before finishing with 11 points while Tristan Thompson added a game-high 10 rebounds to go along with nine. The win put Cleveland in a position to close out the series and earn a second straight trip to the NBA Finals with a Game 6 win in Toronto.

"Before we get started, I know Kevin didn't play in the fourth quarter," Tyronn Lue joked during his postgame press conference. "So you don't have to ask about it." The Cavaliers head coach would later add that he never lost faith in Love despite two fourth-quarter benchings and continued to tell him to keep letting it fly offensively. "His confidence never wavered. He knew exactly what he had to do. I just want Kevin to continue to be aggressive. I don't care about missed shots, take your shots when you have them and just be aggressive. That's what he did tonight and he set the tone for us early." ■

Raptors forward Luis Scola trails Kevin Love as he drives to the basket. Love had a strong game with 25 points on 8-of-10 shooting from the floor.

EASTERN CONFERENCE FINALS

GAME 6: CAVALIERS 113, RAPTORS 87

May 27, 2016 • Toronto, Ontario

BACK TO THE FINALS

LeBron Drops 33 Points, Sends Cavs to 2nd Straight NBA Finals

As the clock expired on a 113-87 victory to eliminate the Toronto Raptors in Game 6 of the Eastern Conference Finals, LeBron James and the Cleveland Cavaliers had arrived on the precipice of destiny. In some ways, they'd been here before, advancing to the NBA Finals for the second straight season and third time in franchise history. For James, it would also mark his sixth straight appearance on basketball's biggest stage and seventh overall. But for the superstar born in Northeast Ohio, and a community who cherishes his place as the greatest player of a generation more than anywhere else, this time it felt undeniably different.

"This city has been craving for a championship," coach Tyronn Lue said, in reference to the 52 years that separated Cleveland from its last title. "We have the right team, and we have the right talent. The way we've been playing basketball and trusting one and another, coming together as a unit, guys understand what we have ahead of us."

This collection of Cavaliers, featuring a healthy version of Kevin Love and Kyrie Irving, helped enable James to turn in the most efficient conference finals performance of his career, shooting 62.2 percent from the floor for the series while averaging 26 points,

8.5 rebounds and 6.7 assists. Love shot 45 percent from three against Toronto, averaging 15.2 points while Kyrie Irving tossed in just over 24. Flanked by a collection of team-first players who execute their respective roles with pride and precision, this was the deepest, healthiest and most talented Cavaliers team ever assembled. James was well aware of the unique opportunity that now presented.

"I know our city deserves it, our fans deserve it," James said of the ultimate goal of delivering an NBA championship to Cleveland. "But that gives us no sense of entitlement. We've still got to go out and do it. We've still got to go out and prove ourselves, and be as great as we can be every single night we hit the floor. So we look forward to the challenge."

Coach Lue challenged James to leave nothing to chance in Game 6, denying the Raptors any glimmer of hope by closing the door on their season from the opening tip. He responded with a vintage scoring performance, keyed by 14 first quarter points before finishing with a game-high 33. Irving used a 50 percent shooting effort to add 30 in support of the King, while Love posted a 20-point, 12-rebound double double.

"We needed LeBron to set the tone for us early, and I thought he did that," Lue added following the

Kyrie Irving sails past Raptors center Jonas Valanciunas during the Cavs' 113-87 series-clinching win. Irving finished with a terrific all-around game, tallying 30 points and nine assists.

decisive victory in Toronto. "Then, we slowly brought Kyrie along and we slowly brought Kevin along. With LeBron expending so much energy in that first quarter just trying to get us off to a great start, Kyrie and Kevin just brought us home."

After a high-flying second-quarter finish that extended the Cavaliers' lead to 44-33, James exchanged words with Toronto recording artist and Raptors ambassador, Drake, who was seated courtside throughout the series. The Canadian rapper posted pictures on Instagram mocking James and Irving after the two losses, but on this night he'd be afforded no such opportunity.

The Cavaliers led by 14 at halftime before building a 21-point lead in the third quarter. Kyle Lowry (35 points) and DeMar DeRozan (20 points) would help cut that lead to 10 following a DeRozan jumper with 10:23 remaining, but that's as close as they'd get. James responded with six points to spark a 14-3 run that pushed the lead to 21 before retiring with six minutes remaining. J.R. Smith added five threes for Cleveland, on a night where they hit 17 of 31 from deep while leading by as many as 26 on their way back to the NBA Finals.

"I didn't appreciate last year, myself personally, getting to the Finals," James said after securing the Eastern Conference title. "Just so much was going on in my mind, knowing that Kev was out for the rest of the season, knowing that Ky was dealing with injuries all the way from the first round. I just didn't appreciate it. It's definitely a different feeling. Having these guys at full strength, having our team at full strength, and the way I feel personally, I appreciate this moment." ■

LeBron James attacks the basket and Raptors forward Patrick Patterson. LeBron powered the Cavs with 33 points and was instrumental in securing their second straight NBA Finals appearance.

LeBron excitingly celebrates clinching another trip to NBA Finals with teammate J.R. Smith.